MUGGED BY THE STATE

MUGGED BY THE STATE

Outrageous Government Assaults
on Ordinary People and Their Property

Randall Fitzgerald

A Cato Institute Book

Since 1947
**REGNERY
PUBLISHING, INC.**
An Eagle Publishing Company • Washington, DC

Library of Congress Cataloging-in-Publication Data
Fitzgerald, Randall.
Mugged by the State : outrageous assaults on ordinary people and their property / Randall Fitzgerald. p. cm.

ISBN 0-89526-102-2
1. Right of property—United States—Case studies. 2. Justice, Administration of—United States—Case studies. I. Title.
JC605.F58 2003
323.4'6'0973—dc22

2003020463

Published in the United States by
Regnery Publishing, Inc.
An Eagle Publishing Company
One Massachusetts Avenue, NW
Washington, DC 20001

Visit us at www.regnery.com

Distributed to the trade by
National Book Network
4720-A Boston Way
Lanham, MD 20706

Printed on acid-free paper

Manufactured in the United States of America

10 9 8 7 6 5 4 3 2 1

Books are available in quantity for promotional or premium use. Write to Director of Special Sales, Regnery Publishing, Inc., One Massachusetts Avenue, NW, Washington, DC 20001, for information on discounts and terms, or call (202) 216-0600.

CONTENTS

INTRODUCTION
It Could Happen to You

OFF IN THE DISTANCE CAME the thump-thump of a helicopter's rotor blades. At first I failed to connect this sound to the interview I was conducting with the young northern California couple. We were sitting in their wine company office, overlooking their lush vineyard, discussing how the U.S. Army Corps of Engineers had brought criminal charges against them for allegedly harming wetlands while cultivating a portion of their farmland. A retired Army Corps official who helped write the wetlands regulations had personally inspected the vineyard and found that it did not violate the law. Despite this exonerating testimony, the corps and the U.S. Justice Department continued its crusade against the couple, apparently seeking a legal precedent to expand the corps' regulatory authority and intimidate landowners who might otherwise challenge the agency.

During our conversation the couple related, in the matter-of-fact tone of farmers commenting on the weather, how black helicopters routinely hovered over their house and property to spy on them. My reaction, I must confess, was mixed disbelief with silent ridicule. It was the spring of 1995, and for years I had heard apocryphal stories from fevered conspiracy theorists about the federal government using black helicopters to harass innocent Americans, supposedly to advance some sinister design for global domination. But the sound of this helicopter approaching, while it had not yet shaken my skepticism, did prompt me to mentally note the curious timing of the couple's accusation about spies in the sky.

Then the thump-thump became a roar directly over us. I rushed to a window and looked up as a huge helicopter with U.S. Army markings passed into view from above the house, heading slowly eastward and apparently traced an outline of the couple's 350 acres. I stood transfixed, numbed by surprise, as my hosts continued talking nonchalantly, pointing out how the helicopter would turn south once it reached a river skirting the edge of their property line. Sure enough, the large black craft maneuvered just as they predicted.

"How long has this been going on?" I asked.

"Just about every day for months," the husband replied. "Ever since the government filed its criminal complaint against us."

Later, when I raised questions with army officials about why they would use military resources in this manner, I was told that the helicopter crews needed to put in their flying time, so aerial surveillance of property regulated by the Corps of Engineers became one of their collateral missions. The surveillance was supposed to detect any alteration of wetlands and provide aerial photos for the U.S. Attorney's Office in San Francisco as part of its prosecution.

This case never went to trial—the federal government dropped all criminal charges due to insufficient evidence. Yet the army helicopter flyovers continued periodically for months afterward, presumably to monitor the couple's compliance with the law, though the real impact of this spying was psychological. The couple and their five children had been traumatized by the military overflights and by the sustained campaign of harassment conducted by three federal agencies—the Army Corps, Justice Department, and the FBI—which interrogated their friends and business associates and threatened the family with imprisonment and financial ruin.

Though my introduction to the Army Corps' overkill tactics did not transform me into a conspiracy theorist, the experience did give me a greater appreciation for the legitimacy of public resentment and suspicion that this agency, and other regulatory agencies wielding arbitrary power, have cultivated among average Americans. A clue to the depth of this feeling about government's role came four months after the terrorist incidents of September 11, 2001, when I read about a national public opinion survey conducted in an attempt to measure whether Americans trusted public institutions more than before the events of September 11. Trust levels had risen sharply for the military, as might have been predicted, but for most other agencies of government, nearly two-thirds of the people surveyed—the same numbers as before the terrorist attacks—expressed a general mistrust for government's actions and motives.

What accounts for this deep-rooted, even passionate skepticism about the role of government in people's lives? Sociologists and historians like to point to our nation's traditions and explain the attitude away as merely a reflexive, stubborn individualism, or worse yet, try to claim it is a distortion in our collective psyche caused by self-centered capitalism. My own view is much more pragmatic. For the most part, people are simply forming opinions according to their own direct experience, or based on the experience of someone they know, with the agencies, employees, and policies of government at all levels of our society.

Ponder this question yourself for a moment. Have you ever known or heard of people like the California grape-growing family who, through no real fault of their own, fell victim to institutional forces beyond their control and as a consequence, suffered serious financial losses, sustained hardship, and emotional suffering? I have encountered such persons countless times during my three decades as a journalist. While some of their faces and names and stories may have blurred in my memory, the emotional impact of what they endured, the sheer intensity of their confusion, anger and helplessness, can neither be forgotten nor easily forgiven.

During the 1990s one of my regular assignments for *Reader's Digest* was to research and write a human-interest series called "Mugged By The Law." Each article profiled three or four persons who had innocently run afoul of federal, state, or local government laws and regulations. These were ordinary Americans subjected to extraordinary pressures. Homeowners, landowners, small-business owners, aspiring entrepreneurs, even people driving along a highway or hiking a wilderness trail, were transformed overnight into victims by insensitive bureaucracies, and by policies that defy fairness and common sense.

We should not find ourselves surprised that such stories have proliferated. Government regulations affect our lives in myriad ways, from how we perform our jobs and operate our businesses to how we use our land and personal property. At the federal level, every law passed by the U.S. Congress is later reinforced by regulations issued by the federal agency administering the law. In turn, each regulation carries with it reams of explanations and supplements. A similar, though usually somewhat less complicated, process accompanies laws and ordinances passed by state and local governments. Regulatory costs to society imposed by all of these levels of control certainly approach, if not exceed, the total burden of federal and state taxation. Federal regulatory costs alone have been estimated at more than $750 billion a year, or almost $10,000 for every American household. Add in state and local regulatory costs and the burden leaps to $20,000 per household.

Once a new regulation is written by any one of the fifty-nine federal agencies, it is printed in the Federal Register and then goes into the Code of Federal Regulations, which takes up more than twenty-two feet of library shelf space. No one has calculated how many more feet of shelf space would be needed to accommodate the legal fine print of the fifty states and thousands of local governments, but a small library building might be in order.

It is not just the numbers of regulations and their cost that should concern us. Too often the rules imposed by all levels of government are inflexible, one size-fits-all mandates that confuse and abuse those who must comply. "The explosion of laws and regulations makes more Americans potential outlaws," *Newsweek* economics columnist Robert Samuelson once warned his readers. "There is more regulation with fewer benefits, and the whole process grows increasingly arbitrary and murky."

Being a property owner or business owner in America today is literally like walking through a minefield. You never know when you will stumble across a regulatory tripwire laid by government. More than anything, the problem has been the near fanaticism of regulatory agency employees in pursuing legal test cases to prop up otherwise indefensible or incomprehensible regulatory language. If landholders or business owners vigorously defend their rights, all too often these agency employees respond aggressively, as if they were personally under attack, and reflexively unleash the entire crushing apparatus of government.

Common sense usually becomes expedient when government's regulatory machinery targets a victim. Whether it is enforcing regulations that don't make economic sense, or pursuing prosecutions that don't make legal sense, the real crime is often the transformation of otherwise law-abiding citizens into lawbreakers. "All of us want a cleaner environment, better health and safety," argues former Indiana congressman David McIntosh, who served several terms as chairman of the House regulatory affairs subcommittee. "But the level of government regulation and the way it's being administered undermines honest efforts to achieve those goals."

With the dawn of the twenty-first century, government's regulatory assault and its encroachments on property rights, personal privacy, and civil liberties, have accelerated. The Bush administration's first energy policy proposal early in 2001, for example, was a request for Congress to pass legislation that would substantially expand the federal government's power to seize private property to benefit electrical power companies, a move that would enable companies to build new power lines on those eminent domain land seizures made by the Federal Energy Regulatory Commission. This seizure power had previously been extended for the construction of natural gas pipelines. If precedent is a guide, such a federal initiative will inevitably inspire state and local governments to similarly expand their own concepts of "public good" to encompass whatever new realms of seizure authority they deem politically desirable.

As described in Chapter 2 of this book, the seizure of private lands and homes, usually to benefit a single large corporate entity, has become local government's latest contribution to corporate welfare in America. This trend undermines a central tenet of our Constitution, in which two specific guarantees of private property rights appear. The first, appearing in the Bill of Rights, in article 5, says private property shall not be taken for public use without just compensation. The second, in article 14, deprives the states of authority to deny any person their property without due process of law.

A strong supporting role in eroding many of our fundamental rights has been played by the U.S. Supreme Court. In a 1954 decision, *Berman v. Parker*, 348 U.S. 26 (1954), it approved an urban renewal project that forcibly transferred private property in Washington, D.C. to private developers. The rationale of that ruling was that slum clearance constituted a public good, so the ends justified the coercive means. Or take the majority decision in *Atwater v. Lago Vista*, 000 U.S. 99-1408 (2001), in 2001 giving police agencies enlarged discretion to interpret the Constitution's Fourth Amendment prohibition on unreasonable search and seizures. Gail Atwater became the mugging victim in this case. She was driving with her two children, ages two and five, in a suburb of Austin, Texas, when a police officer pulled her over for not wearing a seat belt. It was a minor offence that in Texas brings a $25 to $50 fine. But this particular officer decided that Atwater needed to be taught a stronger lesson, presumably because her two children were not wearing restraints. He arrested Atwater, and she languished in jail for forty-eight hours until she could post bond. She challenged her arrest in the courts and the case ended up before the Nine Supremes. They ruled 5-4 that, while she was undoubtedly subjected to "gratuitous humiliations" and "pointless indignity," her treatment was nonetheless constitutional. Forty states including Texas allow jail time for people accused of minor fine-violations, and now the green light has flashed signaling that the arbitrary exercise of these powers is an acceptable incursion into our everyday lives.

Enforcement quotas and other hidden agendas often create a lynch mob mentality among employees of regulatory bureaucracies. The public muggings that result, with fines generating new revenue to feed the bureaucracy, become a strategy for these agencies to continually justify their existence and expand their budgets. A glimpse at the inner workings of one such strategy and bureaucratic structure came to light in Pennsylvania during 2000, when two lead attorneys for the state's Bureau of Professional and Occupational Affairs, an agency that regulates barbers, dentists, funeral directors, and other professions, made a public defection from the agency. They publicized descriptions of how they understood orders to regularly shake down small businesses that lacked the resources to fight back. The defectors revealed a pattern of frivolous prosecutions and absurd fines. A barber was fined $150 for having "too much hair on the floor" during a state inspection. Another barber received a $250 fine for allowing a Girl Scout troop to wash cars in his parking lot. A third got slapped with a $150 penalty for giving a quick trim to a customer on his back porch.

Few victims of these enforcement actions ever contested their treatment because "doing so can be more costly than paying the fine," stated one of the defecting attorneys, Jeffrey Brown, in a court suit he filed against the agency and its practices. Agency managers pressured Brown and other attorneys to bring in even larger numbers of prosecutions, with a quota attached to the numbers for each attorney, a system that state officials called "performance goals." Under this pressure the enforcement teams systematically singled out people and businesses that were easy pickings and took advantage of them, an attitude that warped the agency's entire relationship to the professions it regulated. "The quota system curtailed prosecution of major illegal activity," Brown confessed, "since these prosecutions were deemed by supervisors to produce too few numbers of convictions [and resulting fines] in relation to the amount of time needed."

At the federal level these sorts of "performance goals" and petty prosecutions seem to materialize with alarming regularity in the pattern of actions taken by the Environmental Protection Agency, the Equal Employment Opportunity Commission, the Occupational Health and Safety Administration, and the Army Corps of Engineers, which have taken stubbornly adversarial roles in relation to the businesses and people they regulate. A Massachusetts manufacturing plant owner discovered this reality when EPA employees were found to have fabricated the evidence that brought enforcement action against him under the Clean Water Act. An Ohio market owner learned the same lesson when the EEOC trumped up discrimination charges against him despite support for his hiring practices by local leaders of the minority community.

Apologists for government activism may complain that *Mugged by the State* merely chronicles "anecdotes" that do little more than illustrate a few aberrations in enforcement of otherwise defensible laws and regulations. Yet, I believe a strong case can be made that these anecdotes show the emergence of clear and disturbing patterns, and from these patterns we can discern systemic problems and abuses that require legislative remedies. Particularly, in relation to asset forfeiture laws and the powers of eminent domain, abuses have become so invasive and so commonplace that immediate and far-reaching reforms are necessary.

Can the horror stories chronicled in these pages really happen to anyone? Or do you need to be ignorant and stubborn and just plain unlucky to activate the forces of government intervention? Based on what I have seen firsthand, this abuse could happen to you, or to anyone you know, regardless of how carefully you tread. These stories of victims and their hardships, the casualties of inane, inflexible, and hurtful policies, constitute only a representative sampling of what is available to document. The vast majority of similar outrageous stories occur so far beneath the radar scan of national or even local media attention that we never become aware of them.

All is not lost, however, nor is gloom and doom the central theme of this book. Until rather recently, there had never been an ACLU type of litigious organization devoted to defending the rights of property owners and championing the rights of aspiring entrepreneurs to earn a living in the face of monopoly power and privilege. That situation changed dramatically with creation of the Institute for Justice, based in Washington, D.C., a libertarian advocacy group with a unique public interest agenda.

To shift the regulatory burden of proof onto government and force it to demonstrate a legal authority to regulate, the Institute for Justice launched a nationwide campaign in 1991 that produced a series of lawsuits under the due process and equal protection clauses of the Fourteenth Amendment. These lawsuits helped open up business opportunities for jitney owners in Houston, cab drivers in Denver, hair braiders in San Diego and Washington, D.C., limousine drivers in Las Vegas, and casket sellers working outside the funeral home industry in Tennessee. Legal targets continue to appear wherever the entrepreneurial aspirations of low-income persons are frustrated by occupational rules and requirements that limit entry and competition. "All our clients want is the economic liberty to make an honest living," says Institute for Justice co-founder Chip Mellor. "Surely government can find a way to give them a chance to earn a share of the American dream."

A second legal campaign used effectively by the Institute for Justice, the Pacific Legal Foundation, and the Defenders of Property Rights, has been to challenge the court system to seriously consider and apply the takings clause of the Constitution—"nor shall private property be taken for public use, without just compensation"—in connection with eminent domain abuses, as well as wetlands and species protection regulations that erode property rights and diminish or destroy property values.

Equally heartening, the stories in this book demonstrate that many people do fight back, even with limited financial resources, and their persistence, fueled by moral indignation, sometimes surmount the formidable odds and forces arrayed against them. That, to me, is the most important message of this book. It should give anyone trapped in similar circumstances a beacon of hope, and perhaps even a game plan, to carve out their own measure of fairness, justice, and common sense under the law.

Did you ever wonder what a legal mugging looks like and feels like? Consider these stories from an ever-growing case file of Americans who have been mugged by the state.

1

Mugged by
THE WAR ON DRUGS

MAGINE FOR A MOMENT THAT YOU are driving down the highway of life minding your own business. Unbeknownst to you, the car you are driving, the one you bought secondhand and just made the last payment on, fits a vehicle profile for drug traffickers being used by the police department whose town you happen to be passing through. You are pulled over by a policeman who claims you were speeding, but obviously only wants to search your car. You have nothing to hide so you give your approval. More police arrive accompanied by a dog trained to sniff out narcotics. Inside the trunk of your car the dog picks up a faint whiff of something and reacts. You are informed that your car is now under arrest, though you are free to go. Of course, you want to know what you will have to do to get your car back. You are told there is nothing you can do, except to file a costly lawsuit. Your car now belongs to the local police department and will be sold at auction to raise money so the department can hire more police to make more traffic stop seizures like the one that just robbed you.

"Outrageous!" you say. "Preposterous!" Sounds like some sort of extortion scheme you heard was characteristic of corrupt police someplace south of the U.S. border? No, it is happening here in America, right now, to ordinary and innocent people who have lost vehicles, homes, land, businesses, bank accounts, and other assets to federal, state, and local law enforcement's legalized thievery.

In any war it seems the compulsion for victory ends up as a justification for using any means necessary to win. Our government's declaration of war on illegal drugs, a struggle waged for more than thirty years, is the longest war in our nation's history. It is a crusade with no end in sight. It has fostered a mammoth drug-fighting bureaucracy extending from the federal level down to state and local jurisdictions, a bureaucracy dedicated to its own perpetuation and to an expansion of its powers. Probably the most powerful weapon in the arsenal of the drug bureaucracy has been its authority to confiscate property based on the mere suspicion of an association with drug use or trafficking. Of course, it will be argued that, as with any war, there are unavoidable innocent victims, "collateral damage" as the Pentagon's spinmakers refer to it. In the case of the war on drugs, however, the existence of so many innocent victims calls into question not only the legal weapons being used, but also the legitimacy and moral efficacy of the war itself.

Your Home Is Under Arrest!

As her fifty-fifth birthday present to herself, Judith Roderick and her boyfriend spent ten days sunning and relaxing in the Caribbean. They returned to the Seattle-Tacoma Airport in Washington on November 22, 1997, picked up their baggage, and were about to leave the terminal when Roderick heard someone call out her name.

She turned and found herself confronted by three men and two women. "We're from the Thurston County Narcotics Task Force," one of the plainclothes officers announced. "You're under arrest."

"What did I do?" Roderick blurted.

"Come with us. We want to question you."

The officers escorted Roderick and her boyfriend into a security area of the airport. They searched her luggage and asked questions about a former client who had once used her tax consultant services.

"Yes, I know him," Roderick explained. "He paid me $500 to prepare a trust for his property."

After further interrogation the officers handcuffed Roderick. "You are being charged with laundering drug money," a senior officer explained.

In the most humiliating experience of her life, she was paraded in handcuffs through a throng of people at the airport's ticket counters and marched out of the terminal to a waiting van. They drove her sixty miles to the Thurston County jail, fingerprinted her, photographed her, and locked her up.

When Roderick tried to hire an attorney she discovered that she had no resources. All of her personal and business bank accounts had been frozen under the state's civil asset forfeiture law. While she had been in the Caribbean, a dozen officers with the Narcotics Task Force raided her home in Lacey, Washington, and held her niece and two children, ages four and seven, at gunpoint while they did a thorough search. The police seized Roderick's computer, all of her business records, and two Harley Davidson motorcycles belonging to her boyfriend. Most devastating of all, the Thurston County Narcotics Task Force and the King County Police filed for a superior court order to seize Roderick's house on grounds it had been used for money laundering, presumably because it was where Roderick conducted her tax consulting business.

Several weeks after her arrest she was formally charged with money laundering as part of a marijuana and LSD manufacturing case against a man named Gideon Israel. He had paid her to prepare a trust document giving forty-two acres of his land to friends upon his death. She stood accused of having known the land was purchased with the proceeds from drug sales, the proceeds of which she laundered for him.

"Can you imagine trying to post bail when they've closed all your bank accounts? Try proving your innocence when they have all your records. This has been a terrible nightmare," Roderick wrote in an anguished Christmas letter to friends. "As you know, I don't use drugs, I don't sell drugs, and I don't launder drug money. I will be arraigned on Christmas Eve. Joy to the world!"

At first she tried to represent herself in court. But it soon became clear she needed professional help. With her money locked away, she was forced to go before a judge and have herself declared an indigent in order to get a court appointed attorney. For the next fourteen months, as she fought the charges, the nightmare only got worse. With her business records gone, and newspaper publicity about her arrest having destroyed her reputation, she no longer had sufficient income as a tax consultant to cover basic expenses. She had to get a second job and survive on credit cards and the generosity of friends to avoid bankruptcy.

In February 1999 the prosecution acknowledged it had no evidence against her by agreeing to drop all charges if she would sign over the trust on the forty-two acres to Thurston County so it could be forfeited to the government. Roderick agreed, even though she had no claim on the property. With that signature her house was released from forfeiture and her legal struggle ended.

Her boyfriend eventually got his motorcycles back, but it took nearly two years for Roderick to retrieve her boxes of business files. In February 2000, with help from two local attorneys, Roderick filed a federal lawsuit against Thurston County, the county narcotics task force, and a county narcotics officer, charging that her civil rights were violated by malicious prosecution, unlawful arrest, and imprisonment. In March 2001 she accepted $100,000 from the defendants to settle her lawsuit.

Confiscation of bank accounts and homes constitutes one of four common types of asset seizures being practiced nationwide. The other types of seizures are cash forfeitures, the taking of businesses, and the forcible confiscation of vehicles, which are then sold to benefit the seizing law enforcement agency.

Your Bank Account Is Under Arrest!

An early morning sun had just crept over the horizon when Dan Peruchi drove out of Memphis, Tennessee, and across the state line into Arkansas. The thirty-five-year-old father of four was on his way home to the Fort Worth, Texas, area in a 1968 Oldsmobile he had just purchased, one of the rare and classic vehicles he periodically bought, remodeled, and then resold. Since most of the private sellers he dealt with accepted only cash, Peruchi carried $18,890 in bills of various denominations under the seat of his car, his life savings from working construction jobs and building custom vans.

In his rearview mirror Peruchi noticed a West Memphis police car tailing him with its lights flashing. He checked his speedometer and saw that he was only going five miles above the speed limit. Oh well, Peruchi thought, at the worst I'll get a small fine. He pulled over at the next rest stop area.

"Are you carrying any drugs or firearms?" asked the policeman.

"No, sir," Peruchi replied.

"Do you mind if I take a look?"

Peruchi gave his consent and the officer spent ten minutes searching the back of his car. Under a seat he found the cash and a satchel of paperwork detailing Peruchi's buying and selling of cars. More officers arrived on the scene with a police dog. The dog sniffed Peruchi's money and reacted as if some of it carried a drug residue.

This reaction by the dog should not have been considered unusual since numerous university and law enforcement studies of the nation's paper money supply had determined that most large denomination bills contain minute traces of drug residue, primarily cocaine. Yet this dubious standard for making a drug connection, combined with the automatic suspicion police have for anyone doing business in cash, turns people like Peruchi into prime candidates for exploitation.

"We're confiscating your money because it smells like drugs," a senior officer informed Peruchi, without specifying what kind of drug.

"You're taking my life savings!" Peruchi protested.

"Carry checks next time," the officer curtly advised him.

Peruchi was not arrested, nor even ticketed on this day in November 1992. In return for his money he got a receipt from the West Memphis Police Department, which deposited his savings into the department's own operational budget. If he decided to return to the county and fight this seizure through the legal system, he was informed that his case would be turned over to the Drug Enforcement Administration. "Try fighting the Feds," he was told. Peruchi no longer had the resources to hire an attorney anyway, so he had to accept the seizure with bitter resignation.

"They treated me like a criminal because I did business in cash," Peruchi told me. "What they did to me was legal highway robbery."

His money had been confiscated under provisions of an Arkansas state asset-seizure law modeled after the federal civil asset forfeiture. Even if Peruchi had fought this injustice and won in court, the legal costs could have seriously diminished or even surpassed the value of his assets that were seized.

Federal asset forfeiture statutes and the state laws cloned from them authorize police agencies to seize any property purchased with drug money or used to facilitate the drug trade, without necessarily having to prove a crime was committed. Under reforms to the asset forfeiture law enacted by Congress in 2000, the U.S. Justice Department, the Drug Enforcement Administration, and other federal agencies are supposed to have amassed a preponderance of evidence to justify any property or asset seizure. That rule can easily be circumvented since "preponderance" is usually defined at the whim of the enforcer. In most states, local police agencies are not even hamstrung with the preponderance standard, and can claim property and assets merely on the suspicion of drug connections, a guilty until proven innocent standard that warps the values of traditional American justice.

For a textbook case of this abuse at the local level consider the plight of a country doctor in Haleyville, Alabama. Doctor Richard Lowe lived frugally in a modest home and drove a used car. Having survived the Depression years, he was inspired to fanatically save and hoard his money, which he had a knack for making through medical work and investments, until his life savings totaled nearly $3 million. Much of it he kept in cash.

He decided to use part of his savings to set up a charitable account to support a small private school in his hometown. Doctor Lowe and his wife collected $316,911—in denominations of ones, fives, tens, and twenties—from shoe boxes in their closet. He took the money to a bank in Roanoke, Alabama, for deposit in an account to benefit the school. Instead of depositing Lowe's money in the account promptly, the bank's president put it in a bank vault and over the next six weeks went to other local banks and bought cashier's checks of up to $8,000 each, credited to Lowe's account.

An executive at another bank thought these transactions were suspicious and alerted the FBI, which sent agents to interview the bank president. He admitted the cashier's checks were his idea, not

Lowe's, and he had not thought the law was being broken. Despite the president's testimony, the FBI and the U.S. attorney for that region seized Lowe's account, impounding not only the $316,911 in cash deposits but his entire remaining life savings of $2.5 million.

This step was taken under authority given by the Civil Asset Forfeiture law passed by Congress in 1984, a key component of the War on Drugs, which allows federal agencies to grab property and assets without normal due process based on the mere suspicion that a crime may have been committed. Lowe's life savings were considered forfeitable by the U.S. attorney because his bank had failed to file with the government the required regulatory reporting form, a cash transaction report, upon receipt of Lowe's money. From the FBI and U.S. attorney's perspective, failure to report such a large sum meant the money must have come from illegal activity.

With the burden of proof on him to prove himself innocent, Dr. Lowe was forced to hire an attorney and go to court to reclaim his money. For three years, as his case was litigated, he had no access to his life savings, and the private school that depended on his generosity almost failed. The impact of this ordeal sent Dr. Lowe into a hospital suffering from stress and high blood pressure. Eventually, after much expense, he did prevail and get his life savings back because the government had no legitimate case against him. At the very worst, Dr. Lowe was guilty of being an eccentric self-made millionaire, and that behavior was sufficient to make him a candidate for a mugging by the law.

Your Car Is Under Arrest!

Five days before Christmas in 1995, Cheryl Sanders of Long Beach, California, was pulled over for speeding on Interstate 10 near the small town of Sulphur, Louisiana. Instead of giving her a ticket the officers asked to search her Lincoln Town car.

Inside her trunk these officers claimed they found a nearly three-inch deep compartment under a false bottom capable of concealing drugs. Sanders had purchased the used car just six months earlier. She protested that she did not know the compartment existed. Though no drugs or drug residue were found anywhere in her car, she was arrested, handcuffed, and taken to a nearby jail anyway for a body search. No drug evidence turned up on her body or on her clothes, nor did she have a criminal record.

"You're free to go now," an officer informed her, "But we're keeping your car on suspicion of involvement with drugs."

She took a bus back to California and hired an attorney. After seven months of legal maneuvering, a Louisiana judge ruled that the city of Sulphur had to return her car because the seizure lacked probable cause. No evidence had been produced of any involvement with drugs. It was a hollow victory because she was forced to sell the car to cover her legal bills, leaving her with no resources to sue the city for damages.

"That town stole my car," Sanders complained bitterly in an interview with me, "Not one city official involved in the theft ever expressed an apology or any remorse."

With this sort of unbridled power at government's disposal, and officials who are infatuated with the idea that the ends really do justify any means in the war on drugs, widespread excesses and abuses have become unavoidably common. These developments alarm even some officials who formerly administered the law. "Forfeiture laws have run amok," claims Steven Kessler, who once headed the district attorney's asset forfeiture unit in the Bronx, New York. "The focus is no longer on combating crime. It's on fundraising."

During his fifteen years as police chief of San Jose, California, Joseph McNamara saw and felt firsthand the pressures that local politicians place on police to raise revenue using civil asset seizures. One day his boss, the city manager, showed him a proposed annual budget, which included no money for needed police equipment. When McNamara protested his boss replied: "You guys seized $4 million last year. I expect you to do better this year." McNamara realized that if the $4 million or more failed to come from seizures, the equipment they needed would be siphoned out of city general funds, which in turn would reduce the sums available to pay for police overtime and salary increases. With such perverse incentives in place it is no wonder that many police agencies have become addicted to grabbing assets and personal property. "When cops are put under pressure to produce revenue," McNamara told me, "bad things happen. Hundreds of innocent Americans have lost money and property because of abuses in the asset-seizure laws."

Your Business Is Under Arrest!

Jason Brice personifies the classic hardworking immigrant success story. After emigrating from Taiwan, he attended college in Texas, and worked his way through school with a series of hotel jobs. Upon graduating he meticulously saved money from over a decade of the hotel work until he could partner with two other Asian-American investors in 1994 to buy a Houston motel called the Red Carpet Inn.

The three-story motel was a dilapidated eyesore. Its roof leaked, the rain gutters had collapsed, and potholes made the parking lot look like a cratered moonscape. Brice and his partners pumped in $300,000 to renovate the motel and in doing so, helped to improve conditions in the surrounding low-income neighborhood.

Eager to do everything he could to prevent criminal activity by guests and visitors, Brice signed a trespass agreement with the Houston Police Department in December 1995, giving officers permission to patrol the motel and question patrons they saw acting suspiciously.

Brice also implemented a series of other anticrime measures. He hired night security guards, required guests to show driver's licenses to obtain a room (so as to discourage the rental of rooms solely for the purpose of drug use and prostitution), and installed video cameras to monitor the parking lot at all times.

Houston police officials and the city attorney's office wanted even more drastic steps taken. In a meeting with Brice several officers urged him to raise his room rates from $29 a night, a move they believed would further discourage drug users. "I can't do that," Brice responded. "I've got to keep my rates low in order to compete with six other hotels and motels located around me."

As if to punish him for resisting their suggestion, police began patrolling Brice's motel grounds more aggressively. Officers arbitrarily stopped guests at all hours, questioning even couples with children. Customers began to complain to Brice that the police presence and the interrogations made them feel like criminals. They vowed to take their business elsewhere. Gradually the police scare tactics drove down revenues and for the first time Brice found himself faced with the prospect of bankruptcy.

Desperate to stay in business, Brice withdrew the trespass agreement with the police department on January 26, 1998, so his customers would no longer be harassed. Within days, police officials and the city attorney's office had contacted the U.S. attorney requesting that he invoke the federal asset forfeiture law. Just three weeks after Brice acted in self-defense to preserve his livelihood, a U.S. district judge signed U.S. Attorney James DeAtley's complaint seeking forfeiture of the motel.

The civil suit alleged that Brice "had knowledge that the property was being used to facilitate drug transactions and consented to the use of the property to facilitate the illegal activity." As evidence, the federal complaint pointed to "32 calls for police service which resulted in narcotics being seized" during 1996 and 1997. More evidence of Brice's collusion in the drug trade, charged the complaint, was his refusal to raise room rates.

On February 17, 1998, a team of U.S. marshals and local police raced to the Red Carpet Motel and burst into Brice's office. "This property is being seized by the federal government," a U.S. marshal announced, as his colleagues began an inventory of the motel's furnishings and equipment. Meanwhile, DeAtley held a news conference in which he claimed the seizure was in response to drug activity on the premises of Red Carpet, which its owners were "facilitating by not taking steps to prevent."

The forty-two-year-old Brice was stunned and baffled by the seizure.

In particular, the accusation that he had condoned drug use outraged him. He went through his records and noted that of the thirty-two phone calls for police service that resulted in narcotics seizures at the motel over a two-year period, most had been initiated either by him or his security guards. Not only that, during this entire period he had completely cooperated with police under terms of the trespass agreement.

Over the next five months, as Brice's attorney fought the seizure order in court, the motel barely remained open because negative publicity had driven away much of its business. The toll wasn't just economic. Brice and his wife experienced bouts of depression and spent many sleepless nights worrying whether they would end up being impoverished and dependent on relatives.

Once government prosecutors realized they did not have a solid case, a settlement agreement was offered. The government dropped its lawsuit and in return Brice agreed to implement a few more security improvements to the motel. This bittersweet victory cost Brice and his partners $60,000 in legal fees. To this day they are still trying to recover from the negative publicity the seizure generated.

As the *Houston Chronicle* editorialized, accusing the U.S. attorney of overstepping his authority, "Good people should not have to fear property seizures because they operate businesses in high crime areas."

A Cure in Search of a Problem

John Clayton operated Uncle John's Tavern, a small neighborhood bar in Seattle, Washington, for over four years without hearing any complaints from the police or the state liquor control board. An army veteran and a retired U.S. Public Health Service employee, Clayton had invested his life savings to renovate the bar and buy equipment. The business provided income for him and his wife, Louise, while realizing his lifelong dream to host a social gathering spot for his friends and neighbors.

All of his ambitions began to evaporate on July 20, 1995, with receipt of a registered letter from the Seattle Police Department warning that "drug activity has been reported" on or around his property. Clayton and his wife took this news with shock and disbelief.

"Have you seen any drug use?" Louise asked.

"No, I haven't," John replied, "How can the police hold us responsible for what happens outside our doors?"

In early August Clayton met with representatives of the Seattle Police and received a "drug elimination plan" with a list of actions he must take, or face closure of his business and confiscation of his property under the state drug abatement law. That statute, passed by the Washington legislature in 1988, had been designed to seize and close crackhouses. After Mark Sidran became Seattle city attorney in 1990, he expanded enforcement of the abatement law to include nightclubs, bars, and restaurants.

Police demanded a series of actions from Clayton—hiring a security guard for nightly patrol duty, locking bathrooms with the bartender controlling the keys, requiring all customers to show identification to enter the tavern, barring from entry any patrons whose names appeared on a police-compiled list of undesirables, installing parking lot lighting, and setting up a video camera inside the tavern so the police could remove the tape and review it at any time. Taken together, these actions would turn a casual, friendly neighborhood tavern into something more closely resembling an uptight private members-only club.

As a small business clearing only $200 a night on average, the employment of a security guard and a second employee to check identification at the door created a severe financial hardship for Clayton. But he complied anyway. He also began implementing the other steps, starting with outside lighting. But apparently he didn't move fast enough.

On December 20, the city of Seattle requested that the Washington State Liquor Control Board not renew Clayton's license. "While the owners have taken control of the inside of the tavern," Acting Police Commander Judy de Mello conceded in a letter to the board, they have "neglected to take control of the exterior perimeter." Furthermore, she alleged that forty-three "incident reports" involving the tavern parking lot, most for narcotics violations, had been recorded during 1995. Three months later, the city was forced to revise that number down to twenty-eight after Clayton's attorney made a discovery request for documentation.

One week after getting the city's letter the control board issued notice that Clayton's liquor license would not be renewed. Clayton requested a public hearing. This delayed the board in revoking his license. At this point Seattle city officials raised the stakes. A drug abatement action was filed against Clayton on March 15 seeking "to vacate and close the Tavern based upon drug trafficking activity."

At a hearing on the city's motion for a preliminary injunction to close Clayton down, superior court judge Joseph Wesley acknowledged being in the difficult position of balancing the "community's interest in combating drug traffic and an individual's right to operate his business free of government interference." Clayton's attorney, Howard Pruzan, made an impassioned plea in response. "Honest to goodness, we want to help eradicate drug activity. Seriously, what can Mr. Clayton do? Supposing that he believes someone in his parking lot is doing something suspicious. He can't arrest them. He can't search them. He can call the police department. I am told by his security person they have done that and the police have not responded for three or four hours at a minimum."

Judge Wesley then signaled his intentions and parroted the city's position. "It may well be that one can't run that business in that location. Maybe that's the answer." Judge Wesley denied the city's motion to close Clayton down pending a trial.

Soon after this hearing, tragedy struck. Louise Clayton was diagnosed with an advanced stage of cancer. Now the stress of his personal misfortune, combined with the legal expenses of fighting a two-front war against the city and the control board, took a heavy emotional toll on Clayton. He found himself distracted, in constant turmoil, and his business began to suffer.

Just before the scheduled abatement trial on August 5, the city attorney's office dropped its lawsuit, "based on the absence of drug trafficking activity at Uncle John's Tavern since the preliminary injunction hearing." However, the city attorney continued to argue before the control board that Clayton's liquor license be revoked, which would effectively close him down. The control board subsequently issued a final order affirming non-renewal of the license.

Several years later and Clayton's attorney still cannot contain his outrage. "The city knew it couldn't win in a trial so it resorts to a backdoor to put him out of business. There has never been any evidence presented that John Clayton or any of his employees ever permitted drug activity. The tavern has never been charged with any liquor law violations. The city attorney's office was willing to say anything to end his livelihood. In my fifty-one years as an attorney, this was one of the gravest injustices I've seen."

Early in 1997 Clayton closed Uncle John's Tavern with six months left on the building's lease. He had to leave behind $10,000 worth of equipment to cover the remaining lease payments. In April, his beloved wife died. To pay for her funeral and expenses related to his legal fight, Clayton had to take a night job as a janitor. This experience with the drug abatement law broke him financially and spiritually. "I feel like my life is over," he told me. "Their regulation was mean-spirited. I learned the hard way that if the city decides it wants a small businessman gone, there's not much he can do."

Property rights advocates in the state of Washington are deeply troubled by the drug abatement program's impact on small-business owners. Nearly one hundred abatement actions have been taken by the city since 1992, most against African-American businessmen like John Clayton. "The law has proven effective in closing down crack houses," points out Richard Shepard, director of the Northwest Legal Foundation in Tacoma, "Now we have a cure in search of a problem. Seattle officials targeted business owners in undesirable areas and used drug abatement as a redevelopment tool. In the process they're undermining our most fundamental property rights."

A Drug Law Enforcer Betrayed

On a Friday night in March 1999, Carol Thomas answered the doorbell of her Millville, New Jersey, home to find two police officers who delivered a double dose of bad news. Her seventeen-year-old son, Rex, had been arrested for selling marijuana to undercover agents from a county narcotics task force. She was intimately familiar with the task force's work because, as a Cumberland County deputy sheriff herself, she served on it and had been on numerous drug raids with its officers.

The second piece of information related by the two officers stunned her almost as much as the first. Rex had been driving her white 1990 Ford Thunderbird, without her knowledge or consent, when he sold the marijuana to undercover officers. Even though no drugs had been found inside the vehicle, it had been seized under the state's civil forfeiture law.

"That's my car," she protested, "I make the payments. Not my son. They come directly out of my checking account."

Tough luck, she was told. Any property used in a drug sale, or the commission of practically any indictable crime in New Jersey, could be seized and sold, with the proceeds going straight to the law enforcement agencies doing the arresting and prosecuting.

Her son pled guilty to the charges and was treated leniently with a fine and a sentence of house arrest. But Carol was not so fortunate. She was told that pending the outcome of her forfeiture case in the courts, she could only secure the temporary release of her car by posting a bond equal to the car's market value, which was risky because if she lost her case she would forfeit both the car and the bond she had posted.

Carol made a decision to fight the forfeiture and that created repercussions for her at work. The forty-two-year-old had been a sheriff's deputy for seven years, and now she was being treated as if she herself had done something terribly wrong. Three months after the seizure of her car she resigned from the department. "They made it so uncomfortable for me that I left on my own," she later explained. "It was hard to work with people who no longer trusted you."

Feeling betrayed by her own profession, she began questioning the motives behind the state's civil forfeiture law, and even the war on drugs itself. "As a member of the drug task force, I was regularly sent on raids to capture drugs, cash, and other property from suspected offenders. I often wondered why we were never going after the big guys. Then it clicked: it was more profitable to go after lots of small-time dealers who didn't have the resources to fight us, rather than to focus on a few bigger guys. The emphasis on civil asset forfeiture is on easy profit, not justice. There is no real war on drugs. It's just a profit-making exercise by government."

She discovered that New Jersey prosecutors and police agencies were using the proceeds from forfeited property to make life easier for their employees with expenditures on everything from laptop computers to medical care and health club memberships. In one three-year period New Jersey county prosecutors had spent over $500,000 in forfeited funds for entertainment at prosecutor conventions, including $2,800 spent to hire the Mr. Peanut character to greet prosecutors and their families at the Trump Regency Ballroom in Atlantic City.

As her indignation and outrage grew so did her determination to fight the forfeiture law's legalized bounty hunting. "Most people just give up their property without a fight," she explained. "The government makes it so costly for people that they can't afford to fight. I wanted everyone to know that police departments in New Jersey and across the country are taking innocent people's property for their own enrichment. It saddens me to think of all the young, hard-working police officers out there who want to do something good but don't realize they are just sent to do the dirty work so the counties and the state can get more money to fund their departments. I decided that I wanted the law changed. I was fortunate that the Institute for Justice heard about my case and offered its services."

The Institute for Justice, a libertarian public interest law center based in Washington, D.C., filed a counter suit against the county, which seized Thomas's car, claiming New Jersey's forfeiture laws are unconstitutional. In response to this legal pressure the state attorney general's office agreed to return Thomas's car in January 2001 if the counter claim were dropped. But superior court judge Thomas Bowen dismissed the government's claim against Thomas's car anyway, ordered that it and the bond she posted be returned. He also allowed the counter suit challenging the law on due process grounds to continue in the court system.

"The state is no longer willing to pursue my property because I fought for my rights," says the former drug warrior. "The forfeiture of my own car opened my eyes to the abuse of forfeiture power by the police. Now I want to fight for the property rights of others."

2

Mugged by
EMINENT DOMAIN

SUPPOSE YOU ARE A HOMEOWNER or a small-business owner
and one day a local government agency informs you that to
promote the "public good" your property is being forcibly taken
from you, at a price determined solely by the agency, and ownership
will be transferred without charge to a corporation or a private
developer. Suppose you decide to fight this confiscation of your
property in the courts, only to discover that a legal precedent against
you had been set nearly a half-century earlier, and that court decision blesses this arbitrary taking of your property rights. The fix is
in and there is absolutely nothing you can do about it. During the
last decade of the twentieth century this sort of Kafaesque dramatic
tragedy was played out repeatedly in a variety of settings.

■ City officials in Hurst, Texas, decided to increase their tax revenues by condemning and seizing an entire neighborhood subdivision and giving the land to a mall developer for a new parking
lot. This decision was subsequently upheld by a Texas state
court ruling in May 1997 that ordered the eviction of ten families who had refused to sell their homes.

■ In Englewood, New Jersey, the city council voted in 1999 to declare a local industrial park "underutilized"—even though it was nearly 100 percent occupied with sixteen productive businesses—so the land could be transferred to a private redeveloper for an office and housing complex that would generate $4 million annually in new tax revenue.

■ Florida's Riviera Beach City Council approved a project in 2002 to condemn 1,700 homes and apartments, along with 150 small businesses, so the land could be turned over to private developers for construction of a commercial yachting center. Somehow, city officials managed to rationalize that the displacement of 5,000 low-income residents, and the elimination of one of the last affordable waterfront towns remaining in the entire state, would constitute the performance of a "public good."

This marriage between intrusive government agencies and exploitive corporate interests means that state and local governments have made strategic decisions that the ownership of home and business property should be contingent on who is capable of paying the most in taxes. Under federal and state constitutions the government's right to take private property for "public use" was historically interpreted to mean the creation of roads, government buildings, and other public works projects. The Fifth Amendment to the U.S. Constitution prohibits the taking of private property "for public use without just compensation," and many state constitutions use similar wording. But from this seemingly straightforward language, government lawyers have fashioned complex loopholes transforming eminent domain into a tool to benefit politically influential private interests. The two legal decisions making this trend possible both came from the U.S. Supreme Court, one in 1954 giving legislatures a free hand to redefine public use as actions serving "public purpose," and a second in 1984 endorsing the methods used by a Hawaii housing agency to confiscate property from landowners.

As a consequence, under the banner of "redevelopment," many government officials now interpret public good to mean the advancement of any business interest that creates more jobs and tax revenue than the business, home, or neighborhood that it replaces. Using this standard, a hardware store was judged to be more valuable than a brake repair shop by officials in Mesa, Arizona, while in Oklahoma City the city council took away 1.4 acres of downtown property from its owner and sold it to a politically favored developer.

Some corporations even actively use eminent domain as a strategic tool for corporate expansion. The retailing giant Costco, for example, routinely petitions local governments to seize properties the company desires for the construction of new stores. In 2001, a Costco legal officer admitted to a company shareholder that, "there are probably dozens" of Costco expansion projects nationwide "where eminent domain or the threat of it has been involved in acquiring land for redevelopment." In some cases Costco corporate officials allegedly threatened local governments, most notably in Lancaster, California, that it would move existing stores outside city limits unless the city condemned properties the company wanted.

This unfair micromanaging of the economy by state and local governments prompted Loyola Law School professor Gideon Kanner, a specialist on eminent domain, to call the condemnation trend of the 1990s a malignancy of "developers spotting good property and getting their friends in government to condemn it for them. This abuse has produced widespread civic corruption. Judges, to their everlasting disgrace, are letting them get away with it."

Just when the tide of seizure battles acted out in the courts appeared to be irreversibly weighted toward government activism, in stepped the Institute for Justice with a series of legal and public relations counterattacks. In New Jersey the Institute stopped developer Donald Trump from using a state agency to confiscate a widow's home whose land he coveted for a casino parking lot. In Pittsburgh, Pennsylvania, the Institute rallied the owners of 125 businesses who were faced with removal to make way for a private mall development scheme. Using public protests, full-page newspaper advertisements, and the placement of ten large billboards around the city shaming Mayor Tom Murphy, who originated the seizure plan, the Institute succeeded in November 2000 at reversing the decision.

Opposing eminent domain abuse fits the spirit of sentiments spoken in the eighteenth century by one of the nation's founding fathers, John Adams: "the moment the idea is admitted into society that property is not as sacred as the Laws of God, and that there is not a force of law and public justice to protect it, anarchy and tyranny commence. Property must be sacred or liberty cannot exist."

The Connecticut Diner Owners

For over a half-century Curley's Diner had been a landmark in downtown Stamford, Connecticut, offering meals twenty-four hours a day at reasonable prices to a diverse and devoted clientele. Its standing in the community seemed so secure that when co-owner Maria Aposporos received a phone call in October 1999 from an official with the Stamford Urban Redevelopment Commission asking to meet with her, it never occurred to Maria that her livelihood and the diner's fate was at stake.

At the meeting commission attorney Bruce Goldberg came right to the point. "We're taking your property and we're giving you $240,000 for it." Feeling as if she would faint, Aposporos blurted out, "Do you want to buy my place, or do you want to steal it?" The session ended with the fifty-two-year-old Aposporos storming out of

Goldberg's office declaring that she would fight for the diner's survival in both the courts of law and public opinion.

Life had already prepared her for this sort of life and death struggle. She was orphaned as a child in Greece when her father was killed in that nation's civil war, and at age fifteen she married an engineer who took her away to safety in America. He died nine years later and she took waitress jobs to support their two children. By working fifteen-hour days to save money, and mortgaging her house, Maria and her younger sister, Eleni, were able to buy Curley's Diner in 1977.

For the next twenty-three years the sisters waited tables, operated the cash register, and oversaw the business as it continued to grow in popularity. Maria's dedication and generosity to their customers became legendary. "People love Maria and the diner," Dee Denton, a customer for two decades, told me. "Maria has donated and delivered meals to customers who were ill or down on their luck. She brought meals to senior citizen homes and to prisoners in jail. She even paid for the burial of customers who left no money for funeral costs. The diner has been a godsend to this community."

So it is understandable that community outrage was swift when the Redevelopment Commission issued its notice of intent on December 20, 1999, to confiscate the diner for a revised appraisal payment of just $233,000. Within a few weeks, more than 7,000 Stamford residents had signed petitions pleading with city officials to spare the diner from destruction.

Taking the diner under eminent domain authority was one piece of a much larger strategic plan. The commission intended to resell the diner and its parking lot, totaling about 6,000 square feet, along with other properties on the block that were being taken, to a Boston development corporation for $4.6 million so it could construct a fourteen-story building containing retail stores, restaurants, and mostly high-rent apartments.

Since 1963, when the Stamford Board of Representatives approved an urban renewal plan, the city had been using eminent domain powers to condemn properties in "blighted" areas and convey the land to private redevelopers. In 1988 the board amended its plan to include several blocks in the heart of the city's business district where Curley's Diner is located. By the time the city got around to condemning Curley's the block on which it is situated had been cleaned up and could no longer be considered "blighted," unless you define blight as a collection of small family or individually owned businesses holding their own against the spreading onslaught of competition from corporate-run restaurants and trendy boutiques.

What particularly upset Maria and her sister, beyond their sentimental attachment to the business, and besides the coercion being used against them, was the unfairness of the city's purchase price, which seemed far below the actual value of their property. Five years before the condemnation, when the local real estate market had been depressed, the Curley's Diner property was appraised at a value $117,000 above what the city intended to pay for it.

These considerations did not appear to bother those officials in charge of doing the taking. Commission counsel Goldberg told me in an interview that the diner and the half-dozen other businesses surrounding it were all considered expendable for a "public good" that he defined as improving the city's tax base. "Our job is to improve the city. We need her location. It's one of the most prominent corners in the city."

Maria's attorney, John Wayne Fox of Stamford, framed the issue much differently. "An agency of government is taking Maria's property not for a school or a clear public good, but to benefit a large out-of-state corporation. This diner is Maria's whole life. At the very least she should receive fair market value for it."

In February 2002 the Connecticut Supreme Court struck down Stamford's attempt to condemn Curley's Diner, a decision that came the same week the court ruled in another case that the city of Bridgeport's attempt to take a yacht club was unreasonable. These twin victories for foes of eminent domain signaled that the legal tide had truly begun to turn against government's unrestricted use of this powerful tool.

The Atlantic City Widow

For thirty-six years Vera Coking owned a three-story house less than a block from the boardwalk in Atlantic City, New Jersey. Long before gambling was legalized, she operated a boarding house in the building and drew upon the six languages she speaks fluently to host guests from around the world. She continued living in the house after her husband died, raising three children in it, and she was determined to hold on to her only asset and spend the remainder of her life amid its treasured memories.

Coking's daughter, Branwen, who shared the house with her mother, was opening the mail on May 24, 1994, when she noticed a letter with a return address for the Casino Reinvestment Development Authority, a New Jersey state agency charged with promoting gambling and other economic development in Atlantic City. Feeling a sense of dread, Branwen opened the letter and read in shocked silence.

The letter informed Coking that the CRDA had initiated action to condemn her house under its eminent domain authority and would turn the property over to a casino company headed by developer Donald Trump. He planned to use the land as a limousine waiting area for the nearby Trump Plaza Hotel and Casino. "You may be required to move within 90 days," said the letter. "If you remain in possession of the property after that time, CRDA may have you and your belongings removed by the Sheriff."

When Branwen finally summoned the nerve to tell her mother about the letter, she reacted with disbelief. "This can't happen in America," the elderly Coking stammered. She could not imagine how any government agency could have the authority to forcibly take private property from a widow living on Social Security and give it to a rich casino owner who could afford to buy her house with his own money.

Two other property owners nearby faced the same threat as Coking and her daughter. Vincent Sabatini and his wife owned and operated an Italian restaurant, a family business, which had put four children through school. Before starting condemnation proceedings against them, CRDA had offered $700,000 for their property, a figure which would not even have covered the startup costs for a new restaurant or the legal fees the Sabatinis had incurred defending their property in court. "I've been here thirty-two years and they want to give it to Trump. I don't want their money. I want them to leave me alone to sell spaghetti," Vincent proclaimed.

Next door, Peter Banin and his brother owned a gold shop they had bought for $500,000. CRDA's purchase offer to them was a paltry $174,000, which they vociferously rejected. "I knew they could do this in Russia," Banin erupted, "but not here. I would understand if they needed it for an airport runway. But for a casino?"

Under New Jersey law, casino operators did not have to negotiate with landowners if they desired their property. The state legislature had vested CRDA with eminent domain powers so it could demand the land casinos wanted. If an owner turned down CRDA's purchase offer, a jury could set a price and the landowner had to accept it. Financed in part by a tax on casino gross revenues, CRDA was established to channel money into projects revitalizing Atlantic City and other urban areas. But in 1993 the CRDA's mission had been expanded to assist the casino industry in building more hotel rooms.

In 1988 Coking had been offered $1 million for her land by another casino operator, and now CRDA, on behalf of Trump, was condemning her home in return for a $251,250 payment. A feisty woman, Coking refused to back down in her belief that the principle of fairness was on her side. Coking's daughter obtained the assistance of Philadelphia attorney Glenn Zeitz, who relished the idea of taking on Trump in court.

"This is grand larceny under the guise of government," Zeitz declared on taking the case. He filed a counterclaim against CRDA, alleging that the Trump project for a limousine staging area had "no valid public purpose" that could support the exercise of eminent domain. In March 1995, a local superior court judge temporarily blocked CRDA's seizure from going forward. But in late 1996 a New Jersey state appeals court overturned this decision and decreed that CRDA could seize Coking's house. "I grew up believing that one's home is one's castle," Coking cried after the decision, "Whatever happened to justice in this country?"

With assistance from the Institute for Justice, attorney Zeitz appealed to the New Jersey Supreme Court. The case was thrown back to superior court judge Richard Williams. In a July 20, 1998 decision Judge Williams ruled against CRDA saying its action against Coking, Sabatini, and Banin constituted a private gain for casinos that overwhelmed any public benefit from the condemnations.

Institute for Justice attorney Dana Berliner hailed the ruling as a huge precedent-setting victory for property owners nationwide. "Up until now, courts have given rubber-stamp approval when it came to condemnations. We hope and expect this decision represents a new age where courts will more carefully scrutinize whether government condemnation of private property is justified, and whether private parties or the public truly benefit from these actions."

The Arizona Brake Repairman

A newspaper reporter's phone call first alerted Randy Bailey to the disturbing news that city officials of Mesa, Arizona had condemned Bailey's brake repair shop under the state's eminent domain law and intended to turn his land over to a hardware store owner. Bailey, forty years old, was aware that the hardware store owner had purchased land behind his brake repair shop. Bailey also suspected that the richer man coveted his quarter-of-an-acre corner lot, but he never imagined the city would or could intervene to favor one businessman over another.

"They're coming after our property," Bailey informed his wife and three children.

"What do we do now?" his wife asked.

Bailey could only shrug. He had no idea how to go about protecting himself without being bankrupted by legal expenses. To have his future placed in jeopardy like this, in a nation he thought respected the principles of private property rights, was totally bewildering to him.

Bailey's Brake Service had been located at the busy corner of Country Club Drive and Main Street in Mesa for thirty-one years. His father had started the business when he got out of the military, and Randy went to work there for his dad right out of high school in 1979. In 1995 Randy purchased the shop from his father in pursuit of a dream that one day he would similarly be able to pass the business on to his own son.

Soon after city officials announced the condemnation of Bailey's brake shop, Mesa Redevelopment director Greg Marek revealed in an interview with the *Arizona Republic* how the city's rationale was mostly aesthetic. "This is an entryway into downtown. What we have always looked at is to find ways to remove these blighting influences." Under an Arizona law implemented in 1997, a property deemed to be in a "redevelopment area" can be seized by local governments and sold to private developers. In Bailey's case, officials had decided that a hardware store was less of a "blight influence" than a brake repair shop.

Randy and his father began scouring every piece of vacant land in Mesa in an attempt to find a suitable site for relocating the shop. "We quickly found out we had no place to relocate for what the city was offering to pay us," Randy told me. "There is simply no replacing our location because it's at a major intersection. It would cost me another $250,000 in borrowed money to relocate. I can't afford that. I would be out of business."

Though the Arizona Constitution explicitly states, "private property shall not be taken for private use," the city of Mesa and other communities, with support from the Arizona Legislature, expanded the concept of "public use" to mean virtually any kind of economic redevelopment, including redevelopment done for purely aesthetic reasons. But Mesa's previous experiment with redevelopment had proven a costly disaster. In the mid-1990s, an entire neighborhood of sixty-three homes was condemned by the city and leveled to provide land for a resort and water park. Nearly a decade later, the land remained vacant, local taxpayers were $6 million poorer, and the project had become a monument to shortsightedness and coercion.

In Bailey's case, the politically connected hardware store owner had appealed to the Mesa City Council to declare Bailey's property a "redevelopment zone," qualifying it for eminent domain seizure, so the hardware store owner could secure a better location for his business. In July 2001, after a vote by the city council, the court papers were filed to confiscate Bailey's shop and land. Adding insult to Bailey's injury, the city even agreed to spend taxpayer money to pay the hardware store's construction permit fees, title insurance, and most impact fees.

"This is truly legalized theft," Bailey declared. "To forcibly take private property and give it to another private party is not the American way. The government is destroying people."

Institute for Justice attorneys, responding to local publicity about the case, offered to represent Bailey, and in October 2001 filed a suit in Maricopa County Superior Court challenging the city of Mesa's authority under the state constitution to take the shop. Three months later superior court judge Robert Myers rejected the city's request that it be allowed a "quick take" of Bailey's property, an immediate takeover and destruction of the shop which would have denied Bailey due legal process in protecting his property. Eventually the trial court ruled against Bailey and the Institute for Justice appealed on his behalf to the appellate court. As of this writing, no final verdict had been returned.

The Mississippi Homeowners

One day in November 2000 two agents of a Mississippi state development agency visited the modest brick home of Lonzo and Matilda Archie, whose land in a rural setting about fifteen miles north of Jackson had been in their family for generations. These agents informed the couple that a new Nissan truck factory covering more than 1,500 acres would be built nearby and the state would be exercising its eminent domain authority to take their land because this project needed it for a storage lot.

"An access road is going right through your property," one of the agents announced. "It'll get your grandmother's house, your father's house, and it'll go right through yours."

As the shocking implications began to sink in on them, Matilda Archie spoke up. "Can't we just move the house somewhere else on this property?"

"No!" replied the state employee, "We're taking it all."

"Then we'll see you in court!" Matilda declared.

The issue for the Archie's and their neighbor-relatives had nothing to do with the level of financial compensation being offered. These families and most other African-American families in the area were among the state's first black landowners beginning in the early twentieth century. Lonzo, forty-five years old, a welder and the father of four children, had been born on the land. "This has been the only home I've ever known," he told me, "There's no price for this land. It's the principle involved. They're taking our land. We paid our property taxes. We thought the state could only take our land if we didn't pay taxes. We never imagined they could take our land for any other reason. That's not right."

For state officials the stakes were wrapped up in pride, prestige, and the arrogance of power. Mississippi had outbid at least a dozen other states to attract the Nissan plant, offering the most expensive package of tax-financed incentives—more than $400 million—ever extended to any automaker by any state. One of the promises made to Nissan was to use the state's eminent domain powers to take the nearly 2.5 square miles of land for the plant from farmers and homeowners.

Construction of the plant would not have been endangered if the Archie's and their relatives kept their homes and the twenty-eight acres on which they sit. The former executive director of the Mississippi Development Authority, James C. Burns, Jr., admitted in an interview with the *New York Times* that the twenty-eight acres was never essential to the project. The real issue for state officials was about saving face. "It's not that Nissan is going to leave if we don't get that land," said Burns on September 10, 2001. "What's important is the message it would send to other companies if we are unable to do what we said we would do. If you make a promise to a company like Nissan, you have to be able to follow through."

To support the three African-American families in their legal fight, the Institute for Justice sent in attorney Scott Bullock from Washington, D.C. "If the state can condemn these homes and this land for such a clearly private use, then no property in Mississippi is safe," Bullock declared, "Property owners can never know when the government will decide that their land can be better used by a business or a developer. We will end up not with a government of, by, and for the people, but a government of, by, and for the highest bidder."

In July 2001 Madison County judge William Agin issued an order giving the state immediate access to one acre owned by Lonzo and Matilda, including their home, and five acres owned by Lonzo's father, Andrew Archie, including his home. Bullock was outraged that state officials tried to accelerate the takings process while the Institute for Justice had an eminent domain appeal pending. He went to the Supreme Court of Mississippi and it ordered a halt to any further attempts to seize the land until the court could consider constitutional issues the Institute had raised in this case. Within a few months after the three-judge panel of state supreme court judges denied the state of Mississippi's motion to dismiss the Institute's appeal, state officials reversed themselves and in April 2002 authorized Nissan to build the plant using a redesigned plan that excluded the family properties.

3

Mugged for

THE ENVIRONMENT

MOST REASONABLE PEOPLE FIND the idea of healthy ecosystems and a clean environment to be desirable social goals. After all, the pollution of our collective air, water, or soil resources can potentially affect both our personal health and our individual property values. The broader social question is how do we measure and define environmental harm, and what benchmarks do we use to certify the point at which damage has occurred that adversely affects others. The following mugging examples from the regulation of private lands, public lands, endangered species, wetlands, and the record of Environmental Protection Agency enforcement tactics, illustrate how inflexible or misguided policies, relying on warped incentives and enforced by overzealous regulators, can often do more harm than good.

Mugged by Private Land-Use Regulations

Inflexible zoning and building code regulations enforced by insensitive or vindictive regulators can devastate homeowners in ways that your wildest imagination might have trouble embracing. Among the saddest and most infuriating of such cases to ever come to my attention involved a Haitian immigrant whose failure to obtain a $30 building permit for a minor repair to his roof resulted in a city agency seizing his house.

In 1996, after hearing about Andre St. Juste's mugging, I flew down to Boynton Beach, Florida and spent several days interviewing him and the city officials who were making life miserable for him. St. Juste had immigrated to the U.S. as a young man and worked for several decades as a chauffeur for wealthy residents of Palm Beach's Gold Coast. He eventually saved enough money to buy a rental house in Boynton Beach that provided enough cash flow to supplement his Social Security and create a decent retirement for himself and his family.

After a severe rainstorm, his rental house's roof sprang a leak. A building code enforcement employee informed St. Juste that if the roof area in need of repair was no larger than the top of a card table, he would not need a $30 permit. St. Juste measured the area and it seemed to be under the arbitrary limit set by the city, so he patched the roof himself. Some weeks later, without St. Juste's knowledge, a building inspector looked at the repair work and decided that it needed the $30 permit after all.

A certified letter was sent advising St. Juste that he must pay the permit and show up at a city hearing on a particular date, or daily fines would be leveled against him. St. Juste never received this notice. By mistake it had been sent to the address of his former wife, and she had signed for it but never bothered to inform her ex-husband of its contents. Meanwhile, the daily fines kept accumulating.

One year passed and no one associated with any city agency ever bothered to inform St. Juste that a lien against his property was in effect. He discovered this fact only when he received a court order notifying him that Boynton Beach was seizing his house for nonpayment of over $300,000 in fines, an amount at least twice what the house was worth. City officials not only obstinately refused to acknowledge their mistakes, either in giving St. Juste faulty information about permits, sending the hearing notice to the wrong address, or failing to inform him of the lien, they spurned attempts by St. Juste and his attorneys to reach a fair settlement that would not bankrupt the man. St. Juste eventually ran out of money to pay his attorneys and even though he tried to carry the legal fight forward using pro bono legal services, local courts sided with the city's right to levy harsh fines for minor infractions and to seize properties pretty much at will. When I interviewed St. Juste I found a bitter and broken man. He could not fathom why the American system he so admired when he arrived in this country had so miserably failed him.

There are far too many other property owners like St. Juste who similarly have been betrayed by local governments that lack fairness and common sense. Take Harold and Iris Stone in Lynn, Massachusetts, who went bankrupt in 1998 because the Lynn City Council, which wanted their land for a condominium development, enacted an illegal zoning ordinance that prohibited the Stone's from selling their auto repair business. Or consider Vinton Erickson, an elderly man in Clark County, Washington, who wanted to build a house on five acres that had been in his family for over a hundred years. The county enacted a series of zoning setback requirements, such as the demand that 12 percent of the land be a conservation area, and that he "enhance" other parts of the property by planting 279 trees and shrubs, until 95 percent of the acreage was unsuitable for building.

The Washington Home Builders

On the evening Brian Bea proposed marriage to his girlfriend, Jody, he pointed to a hill along the Washington State side of the Columbia

River Gorge and made a promise. "That land has been in my family for five generations. Someday we will build a beautiful house there."

A year later Brian and Jody married and began planning the construction of their dream home on fifteen acres given to them by Brian's parents. Since county regulations required a minimum lot size of twenty acres to build a house in that area, Brian purchased another five acres in 1996 from his uncle. After several more years of saving money from Brian's double shifts as a physician's assistant, the couple borrowed more money from a bank and applied for a building permit from Skamania County.

Two county planners inspected the Bea's property, located thirty miles east of Portland, Oregon, and approved their construction plan. A permit was issued on May 19, 1997, but as a stipulation of approval the county listed thirty regulatory conditions the Bea's must comply with, including the planting of twenty trees, each at least six feet tall, as a screen around the house so it would be less visible from the Gorge below.

Skamania County's permit approval then went to the Columbia River Gorge Commission for review. This administrative body was set up by the U.S. Congress after it passed the Columbia River Gorge National Scenic Area Act in 1986. Skamania and other counties along the river gorge bounding the Washington and Oregon border were delegated land-use permitting authority under the commission's oversight. During Skamania County's twenty-one-day comment period for appeals of the permit it issued to the Beas, no objection was raised by the Gorge Commission staff, so the county's permit approval became final on June 9, 1997.

With Brian acting as general contractor, and using a home design he had drawn up, construction on the house began. One by one he also worked at meeting the county's regulatory conditions. Instead of just 20 trees to screen the house, he planted over 100 trees so they

would grow to obscure the house almost totally from the river and
the highway on the Oregon side of the Gorge.

By July 1998, the 4,000-square-foot house was two-thirds complete, lacking only the interior work, when the Beas received the
shock of their young lives. A county official phoned and informed
them that the Gorge Commission was filing an order for the county
to revoke its permit to the Beas and prohibit them from doing any
more construction on the house.

"This has to be some kind of mistake," Brian tried to reassure his
wife, "We got our permit thirteen months ago. The commission didn't
object during the comment period. Our house is almost ready to
move into. They can't just arbitrarily change their minds."

According to Jonathan Doherty, the commission's executive director, the Beas' house was not "visually subordinate to its landscape setting." It could be seen from several vantage points on the Oregon side
of the river. The commission only became aware of this alleged violation and decided to act after it received a complaint from Friends of
the Columbia Gorge, a local environmental group, which accused the
Beas' house and building site of having "an egregious impact on
scenic resources." Furthermore, the group claimed that the Beas had
violated their building permit by constructing a house whose roof was
higher than the height of the surrounding tree canopy.

Six public hearings concerning the Bea house were held by the
commission, and Skamania County attorney Brad Andersen
appeared to argue that "right or wrong," a final land-use decision by
the county could not legally be overturned by the commission a year
after the fact. Brian Bea pleaded that he be allowed to lower the
house's visibility by painting it an earth-tone color to blend it into
the background, or that he be given a grace period so the trees he had
planted could grow and provide further screening. Despite these
appeals the Gorge Commission's ten members voted unanimously

to overturn the county permit, and in a final order issued on January 25, 1999, the Bea's were instructed to level their home or move it to another location on their property.

Though heartbroken and demoralized, Brian and Jody knew they had no choice but to defend their property rights in court, so they retained the Pacific Legal Foundation in Sacramento, California, as their legal counsel. They lost the first round when a superior court judge ruled on September 9, 1999, that the commission possessed the authority to overturn a county land-use decision, even if it was more than a year later. The Beas appealed this decision to the Washington State Supreme Court.

Over the next two years, as the legal maneuvering continued and the mound of legal briefs and documentation accumulated, the couple neared bankruptcy. They had already spent $225,000 on the building when they were hit with the construction moratorium, and they had to pay $3,500 a month for apartment rent, the construction mortgage, and home insurance during the legal battle. On top of those burdens they had legal fees exceeding $65,000. To keep up with these payments, Brian had to work three medical jobs seventy-five hours a week.

This young couple got mugged by the bureaucratic power struggle between the Gorge Commission and Skamania County over which agency should have the final word in land-use decisions. Their home and their lives became pawns in the larger debate over controlling growth. The "close the barn door" attitude of some property owners, those who had already built their homes but wanted to deprive others of that right, prevailed in the Gorge Commission. Many of the commission's thirteen members owned homes in and around the river and the gorge, which should have been considered a conflict of interest.

Salvation for the couple finally came on June 28, 2001, when the Washington State Supreme Court ruled that the Gorge Commission "acted without authority of law" in ordering the couple to remove their house. Pacific Legal Foundation attorney Russ Brooks hailed the decision as a victory for all American property owners. "Certainty and finality in land-use permitting is essential. Families cannot be uprooted to accommodate government indecisiveness."

The Oregon Retirees

Tom and Doris Dodd walked into the Hood River County, Oregon planning department barely able to contain their excitement. For five years they had been working and saving to build their retirement dream house on forty acres they owned twelve miles outside the town of Hood River. The site offered a spectacular view of Oregon's tallest peak, Mt. Hood. All they needed was a building permit.

But after looking up their land records an assistant county planner confronted them with stunning news. "You can't build here. The area has been rezoned."

The Dodds, both fifty-seven years old, were thunderstruck. No one had ever informed them of any zoning change. Tom had quit a lucrative job with an oil services company in Houston so they could move to Hood River and start construction on the house.

"There must be a mistake," said Tom, "The county told us repeatedly by mail we could build here."

"Sorry," the county employee shrugged, "That's the law."

The Dodds had received a series of communications from Hood River county offices affirming their right to build. In a January 24, 1984, notice, for example, the Hood River County Planning Commission informed the couple that their proposed dwelling conformed to statewide land-use regulations.

The Dodds had been blindsided. On February 21, 1984, the county changed the zoning for their property to a Forest Zone, and on December 17 the county enacted an ordinance banning houses on tracts of forty acres or more located in such zones. The stated purpose of this "no-growth" measure was to preserve forestland for timber production. As required by Oregon law, the county planning commission published six notices in the local Hood River News announcing the zoning change. But the Dodds lived in Houston, never saw the notices, and received nothing in the mail from the county describing the changes.

After the Dodds finally learned of the zoning change in 1988, a newspaper reporter asked Hood River County's planning director why the county had never bothered to inform the Dodds. "We are a small budget operation," replied Michael Nagler, "We can't afford to spend the time to update lists of property owners."

Under the zoning code, harvesting timber was the only economic use the Dodds could make of their property. To determine if even that was feasible they commissioned a forest inventory and land appraisal by a highly regarded appraiser. After calculating the expected costs of timber harvesting, as well as the reforestation required by state law, the appraiser concluded that the value of all the timber on the Dodds' land was less than $700. Even if the entire forty acres was clear-cut—every tree cut down—the study warned that "harvesting the timber on this property does not make economic sense."

Now Tom and Doris were truly devastated. They had invested $33,000 of their savings in a property that zoning had devalued to less than $700. "We've squandered our nest egg on a beautiful place to have a picnic," Tom observed with bitter humor.

The Dodds would have been happy to give the state of Oregon thirty-nine of their acres if they could have built on the remaining one acre. But since their land was now zoned as a forty-acre lot, they could only sell it all at once as a single plot, which was a ludicrous option since no one would buy land useable for nothing more than a picnic. Equally infuriating was the manner in which the rezoning had unfairly singled them out. Between 1984 and 1991 the county allowed thirty-four other homes to be built in the forest zone near the Dodd property because each of these parcels was less than forty acres. Under the regulations a family that owned thirty-nine acres next door to the Dodds could build their home while the Dodds were prevented from doing so.

On December 20, 1990, the county planning director denied the Dodds' application for land-use permits, variances, and zone changes. When the county planning commission later affirmed that decision, the Dodds appealed to the Oregon Land Use Board of Appeals, and lost again. They appealed that decision to the Oregon Court of Appeals, and then to the Oregon Supreme Court, losing each time. Meanwhile, with help from the Pacific Legal Foundation based in Sacramento, California, they filed suit in federal court charging that under the Fifth and Fourteenth Amendments to the U.S. Constitution their land's value had been taken by Hood River County illegally and without compensation.

On June 29, 1995, the U.S. Court of Appeals for the Ninth Circuit ruled that the Dodds should be given a trial in federal court on their claim of damages. Before the trial could occur, the Hood River County Planning Commission reversed itself, voting on June 26, 1996, to approve the Dodds' plan to build their home. That still left them with several years of bureaucratic struggle just to acquire the local building permits that were required.

The Dodds claim for damages went nowhere. A federal district court judge in Portland, Oregon, ruled that no taking had occurred because was still some value, even if just $700 worth, remaining for the Dodds if they harvested the trees on their land. The Court of Appeals for the Ninth Circuit later affirmed this decision, and the Pacific Legal Foundation's 1998 application for U.S. Supreme Court review of the case was denied.

"The little guy stands virtually no chance against the land-use bureaucracy," Dodd observed in an interview with me, "We may have won the right to build, but my wife and I still had over a decade of our retirement years stolen from us."

The Lake Tahoe Widow

Intending to build a retirement home, Bernadine Suitum and her husband traded their Sacramento house for a half-acre lot in a residential subdivision about one mile east of Lake Tahoe in Incline Village, Nevada. Before their dream home could be built on the lot, a health crisis intervened. Over the next decade Mr. Suitum went in and out of hospitals battling brain cancer before finally succumbing to the disease.

During his illness Suitum told his wife, "Hon, keep on going. Build the house, and I'll be with you." She vowed to fulfill his dying wish.

Mrs. Suitum could not afford to submit a land-use application to build her house, a 1,800-square-foot A-frame, until 1989. Approval by the Tahoe Regional Planning Agency, a state and federal governmental compact that oversees development in the area, seemed to be just a formality. Suitum's lot was the last vacant one in a fully developed neighborhood, and her land was surrounded on three sides by homes similar to what she had planned.

Several agency staffers visited Suitum's lot and did some digging around. Based on the presence of a few particular types of plants, and a ditch near the back of her property line, they declared her land to be in a "stream environment zone," which meant that regulations governing development prevented any construction on the lot. The agency's counsel claimed Suitum's lot should be kept vacant because it filtered storm runoff from the neighboring developed lots and channeled the water to an adjacent street.

The only compensation TRPA offered Suitum was something called transferable development rights. Under the agency's complex maze of regulations, Suitum could sell 183 square feet of "land coverage," an area about the size of a bedroom in her proposed house, to an owner of a "receiving parcel with acceptable use and density eligibility." Once she got a legal interpretation of this bureaucratic mumbo jumbo, she learned that her lot, valued by real estate agents at up to $200,000, had been rendered virtually useless and worthless by the regulation.

Regulators wanted Suitum, who was eighty-two years old, frail, and confined to a wheelchair, to shop her so-called transferable development rights to other property owners around Lake Tahoe who needed the variances to ease restrictions that the agency had placed on their lots. Even if she had found buyers, the value of her development rights was negligible, and she still would not have been allowed to build anything on her lot. An estimated 1,000 other property owners around Lake Tahoe similarly fell under the regulation's reach and could not build on or develop their lots.

"They've taken away a part of my life from me," Suitum concluded in conversations with relatives, "I'm a fighter. Everything I've gotten in life I've had to fight for. I have to go through with this. It was my husband's wish and my wish."

Attorneys with the Pacific Legal Foundation in Sacramento, where Suitum lived with her daughter, came to her defense with a lawsuit. "The Planning Agency is imposing a menagerie of unreasonable restrictions to prevent Mrs. Suitum from making beneficial use of her land," said attorney R. S. Radford, "She has done nothing wrong. She hasn't violated any permit requirements. She hasn't violated any environmental laws. She hasn't harmed any sensitive wetlands or endangered species. She hasn't done anything except apply for a permit to build one modest home on her vacant lot. This is a classic case of government 'robbing Peter to pay Paul.'"

PLF's lawsuit in federal court charged that the regulation victimizing Suitum was a violation of the Fifth Amendment's prohibition on government taking private property without "just compensation." A district court judge and the U.S. Court of Appeals for the Ninth Circuit both rejected the argument, claiming that Mrs. Suitum should have first tried to sell her "development rights," in which she still had some economic value, before filing a takings claim.

The PLF filed an appeal with the U.S. Supreme Court. During oral arguments before the Court in February 1997, Mrs. Suitum watched from her wheelchair as the justices voiced sympathy for her plight. "My goodness, why not give this poor elderly woman the right to go to court and seek just compensation for a taking," asked Justice Sandra Day O'Connor. Four months later, in a landmark decision, a unanimous Court ruled that the lower courts had erred in refusing to allow Suitum to seek damages. Radford, the PLF attorney who argued her case before the Court, was jubilant. "This court decision is a monumental victory for American property owners who are too often forced to absorb the entire costs of a regulatory agency's good intentions."

Any celebration, however, turned out to be premature. In an unrelated case, the Court of Appeals for the Ninth Circuit once again struck a blow against Lake Tahoe property rights when it ruled on June 15, 2000, that landowners in the Tahoe area prevented from building homes on their lots are not entitled to compensation. In this instance the TRPA had placed a four-and-a-half-year moratorium on virtually all private construction near the lake. Ignoring the thrust of the Supreme Court's reasoning in the Suitum case, the Court of Appeals for the Ninth Circuit asserted that "an interim" prohibition on construction enacted by the TRPA was not the sort of temporary taking which the Supreme Court had in mind when it said Suitum might require compensation under the Constitution. This put landowners and the PLF back to square one before the U.S. Supreme Court.

Meanwhile, as a result of a decade having been consumed by the process of court filings and appeals, Mrs. Suitum will literally never see her beloved dream house built on her lot near the shores of beautiful Lake Tahoe. Disease had robbed Suitum of her eyesight during the protracted legal battle.

Mugged by Public Land-Use Regulations

The South Dakota Fossil Hunters

About 7:30 a.m. a raiding party of nine armed FBI agents and two dozen officers from six other federal, state, and local government agencies moved into position surrounding the Black Hills Institute of Geological Research in Hill City, South Dakota. Inside the converted city auditorium, the research institute's co-owner Neal Larson, thirty-eight years old, busily chipped rock from a dinosaur fossil.

Larson heard a commotion and looked up to find his building swarming with armed men engaged in the roundup of the twenty employees. "We have a warrant to search this building," an FBI agent informed Larson, as he stood watching in stunned silence, "We've come to seize the dinosaur named Sue and all your records."

Sue was the largest, most complete and best-preserved Tyrannosaurus Rex skeleton in the history of world fossil excavation. Named after the Black Hills Institute staffer who found it on a ranch in central South Dakota, Sue had been forty-one feet long with dagger-like teeth the size of bananas when she died 65 million years ago. A Black Hills Institute team led by the Larsons spent fifteen hours a day for seventeen hot days in August 1990 digging up ten tons of rock encasing the dinosaur's bones.

Now the federal government, spearheaded by acting U.S. Attorney Kevin Schieffer, was claiming the fossil as federal property. The private land where Sue had been found was owned by a member of the Cheyenne River Sioux tribe, who had sold Sue for $5,000 to the Black Hills Institute. The rancher had placed 2,000 acres of his land under a twenty-five-year trust agreement with the U.S. Department of Interior beginning in 1969, a maneuver that enabled him to legally avoid property taxes, but which gave the federal agency partial oversight of how he used the ranch.

Schieffer contended that approval to sell Sue had not been sought from the Interior Department, and as a result the fossil could be seized under the Federal Antiquities Act of 1906, which prohibited the removal of "human artifacts" from federal lands. Schieffer broadly interpreted "human artifacts" to include fossils of extinct animal life. "It is a crime to steal government property," Schieffer told reporters as he posed in front of the Black Hills Institute during the raid.

But using the Antiquities Act put Schieffer on extremely shaky legal ground. How could Sue's remains, which predated human existence by millions of years, constitute a human artifact? In 1987, the National Academy of Sciences had concluded that fossils were not a resource requiring federal management, a conclusion endorsed by then-secretary of the interior, Donald Hodel.

As Neal Larson, Pete's brother and business partner, and their coworkers at the Black Hills Institute watched in disbelief, FBI agents wrapped the entire building in yellow crime scene tape and proceeded to ransack desks and file drawers looking for documents relating to Sue. On the second day of the search, May 15, 1992, sixteen

National Guard troops dressed in camouflage arrived in a convoy and began crating up Sue's remains, forklifting them atop two flatbed trucks.

Once word of Sue's seizure spread, several hundred of Hill City's 650 residents angrily gathered with protest signs, chanting "Free Sue!" The dinosaur was to have been the showcase of a nonprofit museum for the town. Though located just twelve miles from Mount Rushmore, the town received little of the tourist benefits, and it desperately needed the economic boost from tourism that a dinosaur museum featuring Sue would bring. Local children had started the museum building fund with $61.28 collected from a bake sale.

After three days of continuous searching, packing, and loading, the federal raiding party pulled out of town and trucked Sue twenty-five miles to Rapid City where she was stored in a garage of the South Dakota School of Mines and Technology. With her went thirty boxes of Black Hills Institute records, field notes, photos, and hundreds of letters sent to Sue from school kids worldwide.

For brothers Pete and Neal Larson the seizure dealt a blow to their lifelong dream. Growing up on their father's South Dakota ranch, they had collected fossils and pretended to be museum curators, planning for the day when they could show their findings to the public. After obtaining college degrees in geology, the Larson brothers and a friend formed the Black Hills Institute in 1978, to hunt, excavate, and prepare fossils for museum display.

Within a few years the Larsons developed an international reputation in the art of fossil preparation. Without resorting to government subsidies, they supported their scientific work by restoring and selling dinosaur fossils to the Smithsonian Institution in Washington, D.C., the American Museum of Natural History in New York, and other major museums in the U.S. and overseas. Their success attracted envy and resentment within some segments of the scientific community. The executive committee of the Society of Vertebrate Paleontologists even passed a resolution advocating that only scientists associated with universities and museums be allowed to excavate fossils. It is suspected that officials with this organization may have pressured federal regulators to come down hard on the Larsons.

"They want to use the federal regulatory system to make fossils off-limits to anyone without a doctorate," complained Dr. Robert Bakker, a prominent University of Colorado paleontologist who broke ranks with his colleagues on the issue. "It's especially tragic because it threatens experts like the Larsons who've done more for this science than anyone."

The Black Hills Institute had a huge financial stake in Sue. She had been in the Institute's hands for 21 months, and the Larsons had devoted more than 5,000 hours of labor and $209,000 to her restoration before she was seized. The Black Hills Institute filed a lawsuit to reclaim her bones.

In a brief to the presiding federal judge, the U.S. attorney dropped his reliance on the Antiquities Act as the basis for a federal claim on Sue, instead arguing that proper federal authorization had not been obtained for her sale. Federal judge Richard Battey agreed with this argument and on February 4, 1993, ruled that Sue belonged to the Department of the Interior, which would hold her in trust for the rancher on whose land she was found.

Meanwhile, the U.S. Attorney's Office had initiated a wide-ranging investigation of the Larsons and the Black Hills Institute alleging "an international criminal conspiracy" to sell fossils found on federal lands. "After their Antiquities argument crumbled the U.S. attorney began frantically searching for new angles to prosecute," explained Bruce Ellison, the attorney who represented the Larson brothers, when I visited him in Rapid City.

A team of FBI agents showed up at the Black Hills Institute again, this time with a subpoena covering 100,000 documents and 30,000 specimen photos. On June 7, 1993, at least thirty FBI agents and officials from the IRS, U.S. Forest Service, and three other federal agencies raided the Black Hills Institute for a third time, hauling away fifty boxes of records and fossils. Three investigators from the U.S. Attorney's Office also flew to Japan for eleven days in September and interviewed museum officials who had done business with the Larsons. Other federal investigative teams traveled to Peru and Germany to interrogate more Black Hills Institute clients.

For nearly two years the federal investigation moved forward at a glacial pace. Finally, on November 23, 1994, two federal marshals handed Pete, Neal, and six associates, a 33-page federal indictment alleging 149 felonies and 5 misdemeanors. Not one of the charges related to Sue. Pete and Neal were variously accused of illegally excavating fossils from federal lands, of failing to declare traveler's checks taken in and out of the U.S., and undervaluing two fossils sold in Japan. Altogether, the Larsons faced 353 years in prison and $13.3 million in fines.

Their Rapid City trial, which began in January 1995, lasted seven weeks, the longest trial in South Dakota history. After testimony from 100 witnesses, and two weeks of deliberations, the jury voted to acquit the Larsons and their coworkers of 146 of the 154 charges. No one was convicted of a single felony of taking fossils from federal lands. The only guilty verdicts were for minor technical violations, such as failing to file a U.S. Customs declaration.

Seven of the jurors later held a press conference and denounced the government's prosecution of the Larsons, and criticized Judge Battey for giving them trial instructions which they felt forced them to convict on the minor charges, though the evidence was lacking.

"The government did not prove they were guilty of anything," declared juror Cindi Fortin, echoing the sentiments of her colleagues.

By one attorney's estimate the federal government spent up to $7 million trying to make a case against the Larsons. "The government ought to apologize to American taxpayers for squandering millions on this frivolous prosecution," insisted Dr. Bakker, who is considered the world's leading expert on dinosaur fossils and the author of several popular books on the subject.

The biggest miscarriage of justice came at the sentencing of Pete and Neal Larson in January 1996. Neal received two years of probation and a $1,000 fine. Pete, however, got slapped with a sentence of two years in federal prison and a $5,000 fine. His appeals were denied.

Pete, Neal, and the Black Hills Institute were devastated by legal costs of more than $1 million. That is on top of the $209,000 loss they suffered in the confiscation of Sue. When Pete entered prison he left behind three children. The most intense bitterness the brothers feel is for the impact this ordeal has had on their families. "We can forgive the government regulators for what they've done to us," Pete told me a few weeks before he went behind bars, "But it's hard to forgive the hardships they've inflicted on our families."

The New Mexico Boy Scout

Fourteen-year-old Robert Graham Jr. got lost when he took a wrong trail and became separated from the rest of his Boy Scout troop from Lake Bluff, Illinois. They were on a one-week hike in the Pecos Wilderness Mountains of northern New Mexico. Robert carried a small tent and sleeping bag in his backpack, but no food other than a bag of gingersnaps.

When darkness fell on July 12, 1994, Robert pitched his tent in a mountainside clearing and snuggled into his sleeping bag to brave the near-freezing temperature. He felt confident that if he stayed put in an open space a search team would find him.

Early the next afternoon Robert heard a helicopter approach. He packed up his tent in record time and when the helicopter began circling overhead, he waved his arms. For five minutes the helicopter circled before flying away. The clearing was large enough to accommodate a landing, so why hadn't they picked him up? Robert puzzled over this question and concluded that the pilot must have been a trainee from a flight school, and the helicopter would return for a landing with a more experienced pilot.

Hours passed and darkness descended again. Fear alternated with boredom and hunger as Robert read and reread a science fiction book he had brought along. He refused to allow himself to think about the bears, mountain lions, or other dangers of the wilderness. As the sun rose on his third day alone and lost, Robert really began to worry.

For thirty years Herb Kincey, sixty years old, had led volunteer search and rescue missions in remote areas near his home in Santa Fe, New Mexico. Late on the afternoon of July 13, he received a call from the state police requesting his assistance in locating a missing Boy Scout. Earlier that afternoon, a state police helicopter had spotted the boy in a meadow, but when the pilot radioed local U.S. Forest Service officials for permission to land and rescue the boy, permission was denied.

"Because the boy waved at you, that indicates he must be okay," a Forest Service rescue coordinator explained to Kincey. Under agency rules that meant there was no emergency. Under regulations buried in the Wilderness Act of 1964, no motorized vehicles are allowed in federal wilderness areas unless it is a life or death situation.

Kincey knew even life and death was open to interpretation. To escort the boy out of his predicament, Kincey would have to pull ten other volunteers off their jobs and hike eight miles up to the 11,000-foot level of a rugged mountain, all the while risking injury to members of his volunteer group during the 18-hour trudge, when a helicopter could do the job in just a few minutes.

"This is ridiculous!" Kincey told Forest Service officials. "How much environmental damage would be done by a helicopter landing for five minutes, as opposed to ten people slashing their way for miles through the area? It just doesn't make sense."

Forest Service officials refused to budge from their position. It fell to Kincey to phone Robert's parents and explain the situation. Though Bob Graham, chief of the Lake Bluff Volunteer Fire Department, was greatly relieved to hear his son had been seen alive, he could not grasp why an obscure federal regulation had prevented his rescue.

"There's been some sort of bureaucratic screwup," Graham told his wife. Both of them spent a sleepless night of confusion and worry over the fate of their son.

On the third day of Robert's disappearance the Forest Service work crew tried and failed to find him. Alarmed by these developments, and the prospect that Robert's life could be in danger, Kincey went up as a spotter in a U.S. Customs Service helicopter. He located Robert still camped in the meadow. Fearing a public uproar if the media got wind of this story, Forest Service officials relented and approved a helicopter rescue. But the Customs helicopter was too small for a high altitude landing, and state police choppers were now in use elsewhere. As a last resort, a U.S. Air Force helicopter had to be called in from a nearby air base.

More than seventy-two hours after getting lost, an exhausted and hungry Robert finally got rescued. To this day his father cannot understand why the Forest Service abandoned common sense. "Forest Service bureaucrats were more worried about a helicopter leaving two tiny tracks in the dirt, while my boy was left stranded. The state police and rescue service did their jobs, but they ran into a federal bureaucratic wall which needs to be torn down. "

Mugged to Protect Endangered Species

What if a law existed requiring every American who possesses a piece of antique Revolutionary War furniture to preserve the piece in perpetuity? They cannot actually own it, but they must protect it and care for it, at their own expense, under the supervision of a federal regulatory agency. If they fail to protect and preserve the furniture to the government's satisfaction, they can be heavily fined and sent to prison. This is the sort of situation confronting property owners who find part of the wetlands, or a plant or animal belonging to an endangered species, anywhere on their land. Under wetlands protection provisions of the Clean Water Act, and under the Endangered Species Act, landowners must sacrifice any use of their property that might impact wetlands or rare species and their habitat. Failing to do so subjects the owner to criminal penalties.

States have enacted similar regulations modeled after the federal laws. Homebuilder Lin Drake got bludgeoned in 1995 by both a Utah State wildlife agency and the U.S. Fish and Wildlife Service when he bought land near Enoch, Utah, for a housing subdivision. Employees from these two agencies found no habitat or holes made by prairie dogs on Drake's land, but a federal wildlife employee claimed to have seen two prairie dogs scurrying away too quickly for their presence on the land to be documented by a camera. With only the testimony of this one employee about a single instance of prairie dogs being spotted, Drake was charged with violating the U.S.

Endangered Species Act by "harming" prairie dogs and their habitat with his home building preparations. He was fined $15,000 in 1998.

Instead of rewarding landowners for doing good, the endangered species and wetlands laws force them to shoulder the burden of social costs for implementing the legislated will of our collective environmental conscience. This perverse incentive can actually accelerate destruction of wetlands and rare species habitat because fearful landowners sometimes decide to eliminate the evidence before a regulatory agency can detect it. The following examples are of a different sort. These people thought they were doing the right thing, and as the result of being well intentioned, they innocently blundered into the path of a regulatory chainsaw.

The Montana Sheep Rancher

About 10:30 p.m. John Shuler happened to glance out the living room window of his ranch house in northern Montana and spotted a dark shape moving along the fenceline. As his vision adjusted to the shadows, he saw that it was a huge grizzly bear headed toward the pen where his herd of sheep was kept. Grabbing a flashlight, the fifty-year-old Shuler rushed out onto the front porch in his underwear and picked up his rifle.

Over a period of three weeks prior to this night of September 9, 1989, Shuler had lost dozens of sheep to grizzly bear attacks. He had reported the incidents to the U.S. Fish and Wildlife Service and the Montana Department of Fish, Wildlife, and Parks. Bear specialists from those agencies had set snares and traps on Shuler's ranch, but the grizzlies continued to elude capture to climb Shuler's fences and feast on his sheep.

Large snowflakes began to fall as Shuler dashed barefoot to the rear of the house where his 500 terrified sheep were bunching together in a corner of the pen. Shuler had to calm and separate them quickly or they would fatally injure each other. Before he could act, three bears sprinted past him into the darkness. Suddenly Shuler was confronted by a fourth grizzly—the 372-pound leader of the pack— standing on its hind legs from thirty feet away and charging.

Shuler dropped his flashlight and fired a single shot from his rifle. With a roar the grizzly fell to the ground only to rise again and rumble away into the darkness. It left a trail of bloodstains in the snow. At sunup the next morning Shuler and his dog, Boone, set out to search for the bear. He hoped to find it dead. "But if it's just wounded," he explained to his wife, Carmen, "we've got to phone the neighbors and alert the authorities. There's nothing more dangerous than a wounded grizzly."

Three hundreds yards from his house Shuler found the bear sitting up on its haunches watching him. The grizzly snarled, reared up, and charged. Shuler raised his rifle and fired. The bear kept coming. At 100 feet he fired again and the animal fell, but it rose again and continued the charge. At fifty feet Shuler had to shoot twice more before the grizzly lay still.

Later that morning Shuler informed employees of the two wildlife agencies that he had killed the bear. They retrieved the carcass and identified it from a tag as #53/54, a grizzly that had officially been labeled a "nuisance" because it had been trapped and released on three occasions after killing livestock. An autopsy revealed that the bear's stomach was full of sheep remains.

The night of September 9 had cost Shuler three sheep killed and six more injured so badly they had to be destroyed. Now Shuler consoled himself with the thought that at least bear #53/54, the worst offender, would no longer terrorize his property or his family. But eight months later, this bear would come back to haunt him.

On May 8, 1990, the U.S. Fish and Wildlife Service informed Shuler that he was being charged with violating the Endangered

Species Act for illegally "taking" a grizzly. FWS demanded that Shuler pay a $7,000 fine.

The charge stunned him. "My God, I've cooperated with the government fully and now they pull this," he complained to his wife, "It's ridiculous."

Shuler phoned the official whose name was on the FWS complaint, Curtis Menefee, a lawyer in the Denver office of the U.S. Department of the Interior. "I didn't walk into a 7-Eleven with a rifle and rob it," Shuler told him, "I want to straighten this out." Menefee was not sympathetic. "We've already decided this, Mr. Shuler. Just plead guilty and pay the fine."

Because FWS had pursued a civil administrative process rather than a criminal proceeding, there could be no jury trial. That meant Shuler's only recourse was to file an appeal with the Department of Interior. The case would be decided by an administrative law judge employed by the agency.

Under the Endangered Species Act grizzly bears were listed as "threatened" in 1975. That made it unlawful to harass, harm, shoot, or wound a grizzly unless the person did so "on a good faith belief that he was acting to protect himself from bodily harm." Shuler certainly believed he was in danger when he shot bear #53/54. But on March 11, 1993, Judge Harvey C. Sweitzer of Salt Lake City ruled that Shuler had been illegally "acting in defense of his property [sheep]" when he shot the bear and that he had "purposefully placed himself in the zone of imminent danger of a bear attack." Under this interpretation of the law, Shuler could not claim self-defense. According to the judge, Shuler should never have left the safety of his house. Despite the "gravity of this offense," as Judge Sweitzer put it, he agreed to reduce Shuler's fine to $4,000.

Since the FWS brought its complaint against him, Shuler has lost more than a hundred sheep and twelve cattle to grizzly bear attacks.

The implications of the ruling against Shuler worries attorney Steve Lechner of the Mountain States Legal Foundation, which tried to help Shuler in his fight with the government. "The effect of Shuler's case is to tell landowners you cannot protect your property from endangered species. Under this ruling you cannot even protect your life if you're in harm's way. It's a travesty of justice."

The Utah Cattle Rancher

Using his retirement savings, Korean War veteran Brandt Child, sixty-two years old, purchased 500 acres of southern Utah grazing land in September 1990, intending to raise cattle and operate a campground for recreational vehicles. Three months later, as Child rode a tractor clearing brush off a section of his property, a U.S. Army Corps of Engineers project manager, who had driven 300 miles from Salt Lake City, showed up to inform him that he was violating a wetlands regulation under the Clean Water Act.

"Disturbing wetlands?" answered an incredulous Child, "I'm just planting decent grass so my cows can graze."

The Army Corps official pointed to a strip of ground about fifteen feet wide and three hundred feet long where Child had left tractor marks in the frozen topsoil. This area constitutes wetlands under Army Corps regulations, he declared, and under those regulations any water-laden soil, even if it's wet only a few days out of the year, can be defined as "navigable waters of the United States." Violators are subject to fines of up to $25,000 a day and prison terms.

"So what does this mean for me?" asked Child.

"You must restore the property to a wetlands condition or you can be prosecuted," replied the official.

Four weeks later the Army Corps regulatory office in Sacramento, California, sent Child an official notice that he was guilty of "filling" $1/25$ of an acre of wetlands and had to begin restoration.

According to the notice the wetlands bordered three small lakes on his property, an area of about one hundred acres now rendered off-limits to Child.

Since restoration seemed cheaper to him than fighting the Army Corps in court, Child set about meeting their demands. He had to install a culvert under an access road to facilitate drainage, plant vegetation specified by the corps, and smooth over tractor marks in the soil.

Child was in the midst of this work when he received a visit from Larry England, a scientist with the U.S. Fish and Wildlife Service in Salt Lake City. The Army Corps had alerted England that Brandt hoped to make alterations to his property. "You have a rare species on your land," England announced, "It's the Kanab ambersnail. It's not on the endangered species list yet, but we're thinking of putting it on."

Child and his wife, Venice, exchanged worried glances. "So what does having an endangered species on our land mean?" he asked.

Once the species was listed, England explained, Child could not graze cattle or in any way alter the acreage on which the snails lived, or he would face fines and prison. When England pointed out area where he thought the snails might live, Child realized with horror that more than two hundred acres of his land would now be off-limits under both the Clean Water Act and the Endangered Species Act regulations. In August 1991, acting under a rarely used emergency authority, the FWS placed the ambersnail on its endangered list. About 100,000 of the half-inch long snails were estimated to live on Child's property, according to the FWS. They can be distinguished from ordinary snails only by their golden color.

Two months after the listing, Child discovered that nine geese and two ducks had made one of his three lakes their home. Fearing that these wildfowl might eat the snails, he called FWS and it dispatched two local Utah State wildlife officers to investigate the problem. The two officers arrived carrying shotguns. "We're ordered by the U.S. Fish and Wildlife Service to destroy the geese and ducks," they declared. Furthermore, FWS was holding Child responsible for the birds. If any snails were found in the birds' stomachs Child would face a fine of up to $50,000 per snail.

Concerned by their threat, and hoping to have a third party on hand to witness what happened, Child called a local newspaper. It sent out a reporter and a photographer. Their appearance on the scene prompted the two state officers to make a hasty retreat and confer by phone with their superiors. They returned later in the afternoon without their guns and proceeded to trap the birds. In captivity the bird's droppings were examined for snails. None were found. The birds were then released at a wildlife refuge.

Meanwhile, an appraisal was made of Child's property by The Nature Conservancy, a Washington, D.C. environmental group that often acts as a middleman for the FWS, buying properties the agency covets, then later reselling them to FWS at a profit when the agency receives appropriations from Congress. "You understand, Mr. Child, that with both a wetlands and an endangered species you can't sell this property to anybody else because it has no value," Childs says the Conservancy appraiser warned him, "So we're doing you a favor by taking it off your hands."

That "favor" was an offer of $300 an acre for the 300 acres of Child's most valuable land, an amount only one-sixth the $1,800 an acre he had paid for it. He would be losing $450,000 of his life's savings in the transaction. "No way!" Child thundered, "If somebody wants it they'll pay me its true value!"

So Brandt and his wife continued living on land they were forced to keep idle, and could not sell. A ranch they had hoped would generate income to support their retirement years. "We're environmentalists too, who want to preserve things for our children," Child insisted to me, "But we also want to preserve our heritage. What has happened to our property rights? It feels like they were taken away."

Mugged To Protect Wetlands

The California Grape Growers

On a splendid Saturday morning in March 1994, Fred and Nancy Cline and their five children climbed up the dirt path to the barn of their Sonoma County, California, farm. Fred, thirty-seven years old, and Nancy, thirty-six, watched with pride as the kids picked through chicken nests gathering eggs. This was the sort of moment they had left southern California for. But their reverie was broken by the sound of a low droning in the distance. As it got louder the air began to throb and the barn shook. The entire family rushed outside and there, directly over the barn, hovered a huge U.S. Army helicopter.

As the children clung to them in terror, Fred and Nancy tried to shout to each other over the deafening roar. "I can't believe this," Fred kept repeating. Nancy wanted to scream and shake her fist at this latest tactic in the war that the army and the FBI had launched against them over the farming of their land.

In 1989, Fred and Nancy bought their 350-acre farm in Sonoma County, forty miles north of San Francisco, to grow grapes, raise cattle, and bring up their children. For at least a hundred years this fertile land alongside Sonoma Creek had been farmed and ranched. Oats and potatoes were the most common crops grown, and both cattle and horses had grazed parts of the property.

The Clines intended to use the western 160 acres mostly for vineyards and the eastern 190 acres near the creek for oats and cattle grazing. Fred tractor-diced the eastern field in 1989 to improve the pasture, and replaced a defective tidegate along the creek. During 1990 they diced again and began growing hay and grazing their cattle.

Quite unexpectedly, in August 1990, the Clines were struck by a bolt of regulatory lightning in the form of a cease and desist order from the U.S. Army Corps of Engineers. It accused them of leveling and grading a portion of their property that contained "wetlands." Fred and Nancy had never heard the word wetlands used to describe any portion of their land. They were unaware that under section 404 of the Clean Water Act, any water-laden soil can be defined as wetlands and be subject to regulation by the corps as "navigable waters of the United States." The cease and desist order threatened the Clines with civil or criminal action, fines up to $25,000 for each day of the violation, and one year of imprisonment.

Fred immediately stopped the leveling work and hired a land-use attorney to research the law. Meanwhile, they continued to disc other portions of the land set away from the creek, preparing it for grazing and planting, and eventually they harvested oats off both the eastern and western fields. On December 6, 1991, a second cease and desist order was issued by the Army Corps, this time to prevent the Clines from dicing their 190-acre eastern field. According to the order, this "unauthorized activity" occurred in fields "which our historical aerial photography interpretation shows was nonagricultural." Civil and criminal fines were once again threatened.

In January 1992 the Clines' attorney initiated a series of letters and meetings with corps officials in San Francisco in an attempt to determine why the land did not qualify for an agricultural exemption. After months of stalling, the corps finally answered that it had decided the Clines' property had not been continuously farmed before they purchased it. Under a "recapture" provision of the law, such lands lose their agricultural exemption from wetlands regulations, making any farming by the Clines "an illegal conversion of non-agricultural wet-lands to agricultural use."

To further tighten the noose around Fred and Nancy's property rights, Lt. Col. Leonard Cardoza, the Army Corps District Engineer, wrote the couple to demand that within forty-five days they restore their property to its pre-agricultural state. "It is my decision that this violation is of such a serious nature," wrote Cardoza, "that legal action is appropriate."

Desperate to keep control of their farm, their home, and their livelihood, Fred and Nancy fought back. Throughout 1993 the Clines and their attorney amassed evidence from land records, interviews with former owners of the property, and other sources to contradict the Army Corps' contention about the failure to continuously farm the land.

During 1994 the case took an ominous turn. Nancy got a call from a local real estate agent who related how "The FBI just spent three hours interrogating me about you and Fred. It's something about a wetland." Over the next eight months, FBI agents accompanied by EPA employees fanned out to question the couple's business associates, friends, and neighbors. The questions ranged from what knowledge did they have about the Clines' property, to whether Fred and Nancy ever mistreated their children. Mike Hardister, a neighbor who had done work for the Clines, was grilled on several occasions, and he told me how the FBI "made it sound like it was a crime to work or help a friend. They even said they could prosecute me."

A federal grand jury in San Francisco subpoenaed all of Fred and Nancy's business records and tax returns. During this same period the army helicopters began to make their appearance over the Clines' farm, a weekly ritual in which they flew the length of the property and then hovered for minutes at a time above the house, barn, and other structures. It was a calculated game of intimidation.

Fred and Nancy found themselves on a roller coaster of emotions. Their nights were sleepless under this constant cloud of anxiety, and the strain resulted in heated arguments over what course of action they should take. Must they roll over and give up, or could they summon the willpower and inspiration to continue fighting for their land? Their five children, aged six months to six years, reflected their parent's turmoil. They cried frequently, voicing their fears that "the government is going to take away Mommy and Daddy."

Support came to the Clines from a totally unexpected source. Bernard Goode, who until his retirement in 1989 had been the chief of the Army Corps' regulatory branch in Washington, D.C. heard about their case and toured their farm. He found no evidence of Clean Water Act violations. "Everything you did clearly qualified for the agricultural exemptions written into the law," concluded the man who helped write those regulations, "It's a real puzzle why the government rolled out the heavy artillery on you."

After eleven months of investigation the U.S. Justice Department informed Chris Arguedas, a criminal attorney retained by the Clines, that criminal charges would no longer be pursued. No reason was given. "This should never have been a criminal case," Arguedas insisted, "We're not talking about paving over a property. They were just farming."

Though the criminal case ended, the two cease and desist orders remained in effect to deny them the use of most of their farm. "It's sort of like getting mugged and feeling good about the fact they didn't slice our throat," Fred noted dryly.

An insight into the federal government's strategy and attitude in pursuing precedent-setting wetlands cases, and the Cline case in particular, emerged in an interview that Lewis Perdue, publisher of *Wine Business Monthly*, conducted with an assistant U.S. attorney who had been involved in the Cline prosecution. "Most of these people are guilty as sin and so when we squeeze real hard they fold," explained the prosecutor, "Sure, somebody's going to get caught in the cracks. But it works. It saves money, you know?"

The Florida Retirement Planner

During a vacation in the Florida Keys in 1989, Regina Gonzalez and her husband, Jorge, fell in love with the idea of one day living amid the beauty of these sun-swept beaches and crystal clear, reef-bound waters. So they purchased three lots in a residential neighborhood in Duck Key, one for themselves, and the other two for their parents, on which they intended to eventually build retirement homes. They took out a bank loan to pay $30,000 for each of the lots.

Six years later, after moving from New Jersey to Coral Springs, Florida, Regina and her husband separated. As part of their divorce settlement Regina got two of the three lots in Monroe County, and she continued making the monthly mortgage payments.

On December 9, 1996, Regina received a letter that would dramatically alter her life. Monroe County's director of environmental resources, M. Ross Alliston, informed her that a recent inspection of her two lots had found vegetation typical of a freshwater wetlands created when rainwater pooled over lower portions of the lots. Because Monroe County land development regulations required protection of freshwater wetlands, wrote Alliston, "I regret to inform you that the regulations essentially prohibit development on the lots."

Regina realized the implications immediately: Not only would she be prevented from building homes on the lots for herself and her parents, the lots could not be sold because they had been rendered virtually worthless. She would be forced to continue paying a mortgage and taxes on property the county had effectively designated as permanent parkland.

The iniquity of this situation stared her in the face every time she visited the lots. Directly across the street from her property stood a large home with a swimming pool, whose owner had been fortunate enough to build before the county banned construction. "All of my savings are tied up in this land," Regina complained, "This could bankrupt me. What am I going to do?"

Gonzalez, thirty-four years old, a service engineer for a water analysis equipment company, contacted attorney James Mattson of Key Largo, a specialist in land-use cases. He helped her fill out an application for "beneficial use," a procedure enabling landowners to seek financial remuneration from the county when land-use regulations deny them any economic benefit from their property.

More than three years after filing her application, Regina remained without compensation, nor had she even received an answer from the county. At that point, in 2000, when I began looking into her case, county officials did a reversal and decided her lots contain a saltwater, not freshwater, marsh. That entitled her to develop the lots if she paid a "mitigation fee." These fees run into the thousands of dollars, more than Gonzalez could afford, and if she tried to sell the lots any buyer would also have to absorb that "mitigation" cost.

She continues paying a $300 a month mortgage on the lots along with taxes of more than $500 a year. Altogether she has spent over $88,000 for the land, taxes and on legal fees since her ordeal began. "I'm drained financially," she confessed to me, "My retirement dream is gone. It's a shame what bureaucrats can do to ruin a person's life."

Regina Gonzalez is by no means alone in feeling the big squeeze. Nearly 200 other lot owners in Duck Key are unable to use their properties as the result of a series of restraints ranging from wetlands regulations to anti-growth zoning ordinances and building moratoriums.

Attorney Mattson did a survey throughout Monroe County, which encompasses the Florida Keys, and found 9,200 lot owners who have been denied the right to build anything on their land. If the county had to compensate all of these landowners for these regulatory takings, the price tag could reach $2 billion or more, a sum far beyond the county's resources and one that the Florida Legislature evidenced no compassion about. "That's why the county is resisting paying any property owners any of what they are owed," observed Mattson, "We are engaged in a battle over who owns the Florida Keys—the person whose name is on the tax roll, or the ubiquitous bureaucrats who constantly think up new ways to deprive us of our land without paying for it."

Since 1992, when the county commission enacted the first antigrowth ordinance, "the Florida Keys have been turned into a rich man's paradise," as Mattson described the situation, "because only the rich can afford to jump through all of the regulatory hoops to win the right to use their property." He calls the commission's attitude one of "'I've got mine, now let's close the door so no one else can get in.'"

If the land is being taken for a supposed public good, which in this case would be freezing all new development, then compensation would be in order. Yet neither the county commissioners nor the voters who elected them seem willing to pay up, and so it falls to people of limited resources like Regina Gonzalez to shoulder the hurt.

Mugged by EPA Zealotry

Edward Hanousek, road master of the White Pass and Yukon Railroad in Alaska, was off duty and asleep at home when agents of the U.S. Environmental Protection Agency arrested him for a crime he was not aware of and that he did not personally commit. A backhoe operator, working for a contractor hired by Hanousek, had been loading rock onto traincars when he accidentally cracked an oil pipeline with his backhoe. A small oil spill occurred in the Skagway River. The damage proved minor and the spill got quickly cleaned up. As the supervisor in charge, Hanousek was indicted for violating the Clean Water Act, and in federal court he was convicted and given an unusually harsh sentence of six months in prison, six months in a halfway house, six months probation, and a $5,000 fine. All of this punishment occurred despite the EPA having conceded that no lasting environmental damage had been done to the river.

With assistance from the Pacific Legal Foundation, Hanousek appealed his conviction using the argument that to impose criminal liability for an ordinary act of unintended negligence violates a central tenet of criminal law—that wrongdoing must be conscious to be criminal. The U.S. Court of Appeals for the Ninth Circuit disagreed and upheld his conviction on the grounds that "public welfare legislation" like the Clean Water Act does not require criminal intent for the imposition of severe criminal penalties. Ignoring strongly worded dissents by Justices Clarence Thomas and Sandra Day O'Connor, the U.S. Supreme Court refused on January 10, 2000, to review Hanousek's conviction.

Under this new interpretation of the Clean Water Act, anyone can now be criminally prosecuted if, for instance, his car breaks down on a hot day and the radiator boils over into a city storm drain. Hanousek was intentionally mugged by the EPA to set an example and create a legal precedent. How secure can any of our personal freedoms be when an agency vendetta, and a court ruling supporting it, transforms an ordinary citizen simply doing his job into a prison felon? Consider what happened to the following businessmen who were targeted by zealots within the EPA eager to meet prosecution quotas and set new legal precedents, and who resorted to unreliable informants and even fabricated evidence in callous attempts to justify the legal muggings.

The Massachusetts Manufacturer

As James Knott sat at his desk talking on the telephone on the morning of November 7, 1997, he noticed a police officer strolling across the lobby of Riverdale Mills, the wire-mesh manufacturing plant Knott owned in Northbridge, Massachusetts. Seconds later, twenty armed federal, state, and local law enforcement officers swarmed through the lobby and began entering employee's offices.

Knott rushed out into the lobby and found himself confronted by a man wearing a dark jacket emblazoned with the lettering US AGENT. "We are here to seize some records," the U.S. Environmental Protection Agency officer announced. "I have a warrant from a United States federal judge."

After reading over this warrant, the sixty-nine-year-old Knott gave his consent for the search, though he sternly warned the EPA agents, "I am sure someone has perjured themselves to obtain such a warrant from a judge."

Some of Knott's 148 employees laughed and joked with each other when the armed EPA agents appeared. Only a few weeks earlier, actors in a movie, "A Civil Action," had filmed scenes at the plant, and this seemed like another piece of fiction or a bizarre performance of guerilla theater. But the EPA agents quickly dispelled these fantasies by intimidating those employees they questioned, threatening them with prosecution unless they cooperated. Over the next seven hours the environmental SWAT team seized and carted off company files totaling more than twenty feet of file cabinet space.

Just two weeks before the raid, two EPA inspectors, acting on a tip from an informant whose identity was never revealed, had shown up at the plant and done a series of tests on the flow of wastewater into the public sewer system. As plant employees stood by, the two inspectors did litmus tests on several samples of the wastewater to measure its acidity. Under the Clean Water Act, a violation is any measurement lower than a 5 on the litmus test. Initially the inspectors found pH levels as high as 12 and as low as 7, all well within the law. But later in the day, when Riverdale Mills employees were no longer present, the inspectors took additional samples that supposedly found acidity below 5, a result setting in motion the search warrant and subsequent raid on the plant.

Nine months after the raid the U.S. Attorney's Office in Boston finally produced an indictment against Knott and his company. He was charged with two criminal counts of "discharging inadequately treated manufacturing waste from Riverdale Mills into the Northbridge, Massachusetts, sewer system." Knott faced six years in prison and $1.5 million in fines.

In a press release announcing Knott's indictment, U.S. Attorney Donald Stern vowed: "Those who choose to violate our environmental laws will be aggressively prosecuted." The EPA also distributed a press release from its headquarters in Washington, D.C., under the headline: "CEO Indicted for Violating the Clean Water Act."

This adverse publicity had an almost immediate impact on Knott's sales of wire mesh for lobster traps, chicken coops, and fences. A business research firm, Dun & Bradstreet, sent out a warning advisory about the company based on the indictment, which scared away some potential clients. More business was lost when MasterCard suspended his ability to let customers pay for orders using credit cards.

"I found it humiliating to be identified as a criminal," Knott later told me. "I knew I was innocent. I knew I had to fight back any way I could."

A break came as Knott and his attorneys examined the EPA investigator's logbooks, showing the readings of 2's and 4's that made him
a lawbreaker. They noticed the numbers seemed to have been tam-
pered with. A former FBI handwriting analyst, David Grimes, was
hired to study the logbook numbers. Using a magnifying machine
Grimes demonstrated conclusively that underneath the 2's and 4's
the number 7 had originally been written. Someone in the EPA had
altered the numbers to turn readings that were within the law into
violations. It did not seem to be any coincidence that these tests containing altered numbers were conducted by the two inspectors while
they were taking samples alone, without any supervision by
Riverdale Mills employees.

Another important piece of evidence emerged during the discovery process when Knott's lawyers uncovered an incriminating letter
in the EPA Boston office files. Knott had written the Massachusetts
Department of Environmental Protection years earlier about a separate matter, and at the bottom of the letter a state bureaucrat hand-
wrote the following to his superiors: "I wouldn't mind making his
[Knott's] life miserable for a while." Though Knott and his attorneys
were never able to establish a clear link between this note and the
EPA's legal action, the implication seemed clear that environmental
bureaucrats may have had a personal grudge against Knott for being
a prickly person to deal with.

A few weeks after Knott released these findings, U.S. district
judge Nathaniel Gorton in Boston refused to allow the EPA to admit
the test results as evidence, ruling that the inspectors had taken the
violation samples without the presence of plant employees in breech
of an agreement the EPA had with Knott. Even more damning,
though Judge Gorton did not take this into consideration for his ruling, the Town of Northbridge's sewage treatment plant manager,
James Madigan, was prepared to testify that he regularly monitored

the pH levels of discharges by Riverdale Mills and had always found them within acceptable limits. Even if the pH levels had been what the EPA claimed, Madigan said the effect on the environment would have been negligible." With flow time, the Riverdale Mills wastewater would be so diluted you wouldn't even notice it here," said Madigan. "It would have no impact at all on us. I definitely told the investigators. That's one of the questions they asked me." Madigan was never asked to testify before the grand jury that indicted Knott.

Sixteen days before Knott's trial was scheduled to begin the U.S. Attorney's Office asked Judge Gorton to dismiss its case. After suffering $238,000 in legal costs, and incalculable damage to his personal and business reputation, Knott decided to file a lawsuit under the Hyde Amendment, a law passed by Congress that allows a prevailing defendant in a criminal case to recover costs associated with his defense. Judge Gorton declared in July 2000, that the EPA investigation of Knott amounted to an unreasonable search and seizure of Knott's property, and the government had failed to reveal evidence that would have cleared Knott and perhaps prevented his indictment in the first place. "The court is also troubled by the government's unnecessary harassment of defendants and their employees," Judge Gorton wrote. Knott was awarded $68,726 as reimbursement for his legal fees.

James Knott survived the regulatory agency vendetta against him but did so at a high cost. A year after his vindication his anger still had not cooled, though he could manage a philosophical overview of what happened. "The practice of raising revenues by intimidating successful businessmen, threatening them with fines, jail terms, and the high costs of lawsuits has worked in the past, and what happened to me is a classic example of this practice. I was just too stubborn to let them succeed this time."

Public sympathy for Knott poured in from other victims of EPA quotas and vendettas. A Milton, Massachusetts, chemical plant engineer wrote Knott to report how he had been sued by the EPA for $28 million for failing to respond to an "information request" letter from the agency. In truth he had replied, informing the agency that he no longer worked for the small chemical processing company that had been targeted, most of the documents the EPA requested had been impounded by the bank which foreclosed on his company, and most of the documents were already in EPA files. The EPA and Department of Justice filed a lawsuit anyway and the impoverished engineer was forced to represent himself in court. When the federal judge hearing this case threatened to throw the lawsuit out for lack of evidence, EPA offered the engineer a settlement of $1,250 without any admission of guilt from him. In Knott's case, wrote the engineer, "either EPA was just trying to make a 'body count' quota, or you were being targeted for being proactive."

The Iowa Metal Salvager

Forty-six-year-old Harold Higman, Jr. was pumping gas into his pickup truck on the morning of August 23, 1991, when a caravan of six cars roared up along the road to his property outside Akron, Iowa. The vehicles came to a stop next to his gas pump. A federal Bureau of Alcohol, Tobacco, and Firearms (ATF) agent jumped out of one car and leveled a shotgun at Higman, yelling, "Don't move!"

Other armed ATF agents wearing bulletproof vests and accompanied by investigators from the U.S. Environmental Protection Agency fanned out across Higman's three hundred acres, the site of Higman Sand and Gravel, Inc. Employees working at various locations around the property were rounded up and the plant's operations were shut down.

"What's this all about?" Higman, and his father, Bud, kept frantically asking. At first, no one would give them any information. Finally, a special agent with the EPA handed over a search warrant alleging that the Higmans were storing hazardous wastes without a permit.

During the EPA search, one hundred barrels were found which had been legally collected and disposed of as part of the Higman metal-salvage business. But the EPA's chemical sampling also found thirteen of those barrels contained residues of paint thinner or solvents.

"We don't know anything about paint thinner in those barrels," Harold protested. "We never authorized any disposal of anything like that."

Four months after the raid both Higmans were indicted on federal charges of illegally storing hazardous wastes. If convicted, they could be imprisoned for up to five years and fined $50,000 for each day the waste had been on their property, a sum amounting to more than $40 million.

During the discovery process and later, during their trial, the EPA special agent who had delivered the search warrant revealed how a local paid informant made the original allegation of misconduct against the Higmans. That informant turned out to be a twenty-eight-year-old man who had worked briefly for the Higmans as a laborer and held a grudge against the family. He claimed that the father and son had ordered him to remove barrels—some containing paint thinner—from an Akron body shop and hide them on the Higman land.

Once the trial began on November 2, 1992, the informant's testimony and credibility quickly disintegrated. A second Higman employee who had helped the informant load the barrels testified that all of the barrels had been empty. Another witness stated that after the Higmans demoted the informant, he had vengefully threatened to "get them shut down." Even the informant's ex-wife, who had been married to him during his employment by the Higmans, got on the witness stand and called her ex a habitual liar with a financial incentive to get even with the Higman family.

It took the jury just a short time to find the Higmans not guilty on all of the charges. While elated at being exonerated, they still had $250,000 in legal bills to pay, and their business would take years to rebuild because they had to lure back customers alienated by the negative publicity generated by the EPA's press releases to the media.

"The EPA never bothered to check out the credibility or motives of this disaffected employee," Harold Higman told me in an interview at his office. "They charged in here and used trumped up charges to almost ruin us. After we were vindicated by the jury we never got an apology from the EPA. No one in that agency had the decency to admit they were wrong, and that someone had planted evidence and duped them for financial gain."

4

Mugged to
"PROTECT" THE DISADVANTAGED

AN SOCIETY ASSIST AND PROTECT persons who are financially impoverished, or who have been physically or mentally disabled, or who feel discriminated against by virtue of their race, gender, or sexual preference, and do so without disadvantaging those among us who must shoulder most of the costs for this social action? One standard we can use to test the fairness or harm of such well-intentioned laws would be the extent to which generally law-abiding business owners or property owners must struggle against the regulatory system to comply, without their very survival being placed in jeopardy.

Apply this standard to the middle-aged woman in New York City who came up against a rent control law ostensibly enacted to protect low-income people from exploitation by landlords. Pari Dulac owned an apartment above a small restaurant she operated in Greenwich Village. She decided to exercise her right to live in the apartment herself. She informed the tenant, but he not only refused to move, he stopped paying rent. During an appeals process, the tenant used a diversionary argument alleging that records from the 1950s, long before Dulac owned the apartment, showed that the minimum rent should be $30 instead of the $427 a month she was charging because the apartment was allegedly covered under the old rent control rules.

For the next ten years, through the 1990s, this tenant manipulated the city's Byzantine maze of rent control laws, which are heavily weighted to favor tenants, and succeeded at living off Dulac rent free the entire period. She spent $100,000 in legal fees and finally won a State Supreme Court eviction ruling in 1998, only to see the tenant file bankruptcy to deny her any of the ten years worth of back rent. Her mugging is not an isolated or aberrational event, either in relation to rent control, or to any of the other laws "protecting" the disadvantaged, as the following stories demonstrate.

In the Name of Affordable Housing

New York's Reluctant Landlords

When Jerrold and Ellen Ziman and their two children moved from California to New York City, a transition made so Jerrold could leave Hollywood and pursue his acting career on Broadway, their life savings went for a down payment on a colonial-era brick townhouse in Greenwich Village. The house had been divided into tiny rental units occupied by three tenants, but under New York rent control law "owner-occupancy evictions" could occur if the new landlord intended to occupy the dwelling. After being assured by attorneys that the eviction process would take only a few months, the Zimans placed most of their furniture and belongings in storage and moved into the house's only empty unit to await the tenants' departure.

Three months after the Zimans filed their eviction papers in July 1984, New York Governor Mario Cuomo signed a change in the state housing law to prevent owner-occupancy evictions of tenants who had lived in a property for twenty years or more. Two of the

Zimans' three tenants qualified, immediately canceling their evictions, while the third tenant failed to qualify but also refused to leave, and filed a challenge to his eviction in housing court.

Overnight the Zimans not only became permanent landlords, the couple and their two children, ages two and seven, now found themselves trapped in their own home, crammed into a 341-square-foot apartment. The remaining 1,023 square feet of their house was occupied by three single men, aged thirty-eight to fifty-five, who paid a combined total of just $440 a month in rent. It was a sum that rent control laws prevented the Zimans from increasing and which failed to even cover what the couple had to pay every month in property taxes and the mortgage.

Daily stress and mounting anguish began to takes a toll. "This is so unfair," Ellen would exclaim, "It's as if they are stealing from us." Jerrold, trying hard to control his frustration and anger, could only promise her: "We'll find a way to make our case, no matter how long it takes."

The Zimans hired an attorney who filed new eviction applications based on a hardship provision of the law allowing owners a minimum rate of return on their property. Over the next two years, several extensive audits conducted by the State Department of Housing and Community Relations (DHCR) supported the Ziman claim of being unable to realize a new annual return of at least 8.5 percent of their building's assessed value. After each audit an administrative law judge, citing other provisions of law guaranteeing tenant rights, ruled that DHCR could still deny the eviction applications. And that is just what the agency did.

Grimly the Zimans continued filing appeals through the state court system, as conditions in their home life deteriorated and their mood turned desperate. Both children slept in a closet, while their parents slept in the 11-by-13-foot kitchen, which also served as the dining room and living room. No one had privacy or even the space to read without distraction. Their legal fees continued to escalate, the mortgage payments and taxes had to be paid, all on Jerrold's irregular income as an actor and Ellen's modest salary as a school teacher.

Meanwhile, a virtual state of war existed between the Zimans and their three tenants. The men entertained a constant stream of visitors whose loud, nightlong parties made sleep almost impossible. The family frequently found needles and other drug paraphernalia littering the hallway outside their door. As for their meager rent, the tenants often fell six months behind on payments, and paid up only when the Zimans had their attorney take action in housing court.

Three years later the tenant who had been fighting his eviction died, enabling the Zimans to move their son, now nine years old, into the vacated bedroom. Each night the child had to climb a public staircase in his own home to the second floor room and use a key to unlock his door.

Step by tortuous legal step the Zimans challenged the DHCR and its intransigence on every point. A state trial court upheld the agency and its verdict, but in 1989 the Appellate Division overturned that ruling and declared that the Zimans qualified under hardship standards to live in their own home alone. Though DHCR stubbornly appealed, a unanimous Court of Appeals supported the Zimans in May 1990, and ordered DHCR to grant their eviction applications.

Then came more intransigence from an agency devoted to trampling on the rights of property owners. DHCR did not process the eviction certificates for another four months, and even when the certificates were issued, still another three-month waiting period was required before the Zimans could begin court action. When they won judgments of possession for their home in July 1991, they had to wait six more months before executing the warrants of eviction.

Their last tenant finally left in January 1992, nearly eight years after the Zimans had purchased their home.

With help from attorney Sam Kazman of the Competitive Enterprise Institute in Washington, D.C, the Zimans filed suit for damages against DHCR and the state of New York in 1993, arguing that the rent control law constituted an illegal taking of their property. Their damage claims failed at every level of the New York state courts, and on February 23, 1998, the U.S. Supreme Court declined to hear their appeal.

The long ordeal cost the couple $700,000 in legal fees, mortgage payments, taxes, and the loss of the use of their building. Their experience could have been the real-life basis for a movie such as "Pacific Heights," which dealt with a renter from hell who manipulated San Francisco's rent control law to avoid eviction or paying rent. The Zimans still debate what lessons the experience taught them. "Yes, we won the house back, but we lost a whole period of our lives," says Jerrold, who had to give up his acting career to carry on the legal fight. His wife Ellen puts the experience into a broader perspective: "We got a hard lesson, one that could confront any homeowner in this city, about how the housing regulatory system can use and abuse ordinary, innocent people."

The San Francisco Hotel Owners

French immigrants Claude and Micheline Lambert represent one of those classic American success stories of self-starters who worked their way up from the bottom rungs of the labor market. After arriving in San Francisco in 1966, they toiled as hotel janitors and doing odd jobs in return for room and board at the Cornell, a six-story fifty-eight-room Victorian hotel where, except for a maid, they were the only employees.

Dark, filthy, in a state of total disrepair, the Cornell's deplorable conditions were home to twelve elderly residents. The hotel windows were so coated with grime that no one could see in or out, and swarms of cockroaches competed with the residents for bed space. The Lamberts labored seven days a week cleaning and remodeling the building. In 1974 they acquired the hotel's lease, opened a French restaurant in the basement, and began upgrading the rooms one at a time, turning the Cornell into a respectable, European-style hotel. Four years later they purchased this building they had so carefully renovated.

Three years passed and the San Francisco Board of Supervisors adopted an ordinance designed to prevent hotels from converting residential rooms—those that had been rented to the same guests for thirty-two days or more—into tourist rooms for daily rental. The ostensible goal of the ordinance was to preserve low cost affordable housing in the city. To set each hotel's distribution of residential and tourist rooms, an arbitrary date several years earlier was chosen, September 23, 1979, at which time a room usage survey had been conducted.

For the Lamberts the ordinance proved to be a financial straitjacket. On the survey date, thirty-one of their fifty-eight rooms were occupied by foreign exchange students and business travelers who had stayed for more than a month. This meant that more than half of their hotel would now have to be made available permanently to long-term residents, unless the Lamberts paid the city a ransom. To convert a residential room into a tourist room, San Francisco officials demanded a cash payment equal to 40 percent of the appraised value of the rooms and the land. Given that land values in downtown San Francisco were then, and remain, among the highest in the nation, the "mitigation" would have cost the couple hundreds of thousands of dollars.

Over the next decade, because the hotel was not allowed to rent the thirty-one rooms to tourists—increasingly the bulk of the Lamberts' business—the ordinance effectively imposed a vacancy rate of 15 percent on the Cornell even at the height of the tourist season in August and September. Income was being squeezed in a similar fashion from all 528 small hotels in San Francisco covered by the ordinance, as evidenced by a 1994 city survey that found over 5,000 "residential" rooms remained vacant because visitors were unwilling to rent for the required thirty-day period. An ordinance supposedly designed to preserve housing for the poor had backfired and created a glut of unused housing at a time when the city suffered from a shortage of tourist rooms.

Finally in 1990, the Lamberts were able to apply for a permit from two city agencies to convert their often-vacant residential rooms to tourist use. After two appraisals of the hotel, undertaken by the city real estate department at a cost to the Lamberts of several thousand dollars, the department concluded that to grant their permits the Lamberts would have to pay the city a $600,000 "housing replacement fee" for the right to rent the rest of their rooms on a daily basis.

Claude was understandably outraged. "We can't afford this," he fumed to his wife, and their daughter, Sabine, "This is so unfair. What can we do?"

San Francisco Mayor Frank Jordan took up the Lambert's cause and argued they should receive a conversion permit despite their inability to pay the fee. "The Cornell Hotel is not and has not been a low-income housing opportunity," Jordan wrote the planning commission, pointing out that rooms at the Cornell rented for over $1,100 per month. "It is hard for anyone to see how preventing the Cornell Hotel from carrying out business activity affects low-income or senior residents in San Francisco."

Despite the logic of the mayor's plea, the planning commission and the board of permit appeals denied the Lambert's conversion request, though the agencies did reduce the number of residential rooms to twenty-four. According to the commission's reasoning, without payment of $600,000 the permit for the Lamberts would be incompatible with the neighborhood's character and be injurious to "the health, safety, and welfare of the city."

Claude and Micheline Lambert believe with good cause that the city regulation "takes" their private property—in this case their rooms—for the public use of affordable housing without giving them the compensation guaranteed by the Fifth Amendment of the U.S. Constitution. They filed a lawsuit demanding the right to convert all of their rooms to tourist use. A state court upheld the city's right to regulate, as did a state court of appeals in 1997. With help from the Pacific Legal Foundation in Sacramento, they continued appealing their case until it reached the U.S. Supreme Court. In March 2000, by a 6-3 vote, the justices declined to hear the couple's case. Only Justices Antonin Scalia, Anthony Kennedy, and Clarence Thomas, wanted to review the way local officials imposed unreasonable demands on property owners in disputes over zoning and building permits. The rest of the justices seemed determined to avoid cases that call into question the power of local officials to set policies that undermine private property rights.

Only politics and politicians can rectify the damage done to the Lamberts and other small hotel owners. "Half their hotel is being held hostage and for ransom," charged Andrew Zacks, their attorney for a decade. "The city needs to recognize that rectifying a housing shortage problem shouldn't be attempted on the backs of individual property owners. The city has taken their property for public use without compensation."

After more than $100,000 in legal and other bills related to their lawsuit, the Lamberts continue to lose about $5,000 a week because they are not allowed to rent all of their rooms each night. "I just want the flexibility to run this hotel like any other business," Claude pleaded in a conversation with me. "This situation is simply crazy."

In the Name of Disabilities

The South Dakota Motel Operators

At the age of six Richard Hauk got his start in the hotel business as a bellboy at his parents' motel. Even at that early point in his life he dreamed of one day owning his own motel. That goal became reality in 1992, when Richard and his wife Karla purchased property in Wall, South Dakota.

With their life savings and a bank loan, the Hauks invested a total of $800,000 to purchase the land, a Days Inn franchise, and to finance construction of their thirty-two-room motel. They hired an architect and a construction firm with a track record of designing and building Days Inn motels. Following plans approved by Days Inn, they reserved two specially designed rooms and two parking spaces for the handicapped, and built an entranceway accessible to wheelchairs. When they opened their motel on July 1, 1993, they were proud to be the first of thirteen area motels to provide facilities for the disabled.

Unknown to the Hauks, the Americans With Disabilities Act (ADA) passed by Congress required all public accommodations built after January 26, 1993, to comply with regulations prescribed by the Disability Rights Section of the U.S. Justice Department. In August 1994, two Justice Department attorneys and an architect flew in from Washington, D.C. and spent three hours inspecting the motel. "We'll get back to you," one of the attorneys remarked after their inspection.

Seven months later the Hauks received a registered letter from Justice Department officials listing six pages of alleged ADA violations. Among them: even though the motel had only two stories and a basement, an elevator had to be installed; the parking spaces and wheelchair ramp, intentionally built to slope to prevent ice from forming, had to be leveled; and bathroom doorways in non-handicapped rooms had to be widened to accommodate visitors in wheelchairs.

To comply with all of the complaints would have required rebuilding the entire motel, at a cost of $300,000, a sum that would bankrupt the Hauks. "What have we done to be treated like criminals?" Karla wanted to know.

In July 1995, and again in January 1996, the Hauks sent the Justice Department certified letters offering a range of solutions to comply with the ADA. They received no reply to their offers. Instead, they got slapped with a lawsuit from the Justice Department charging them, along with their architect, their contractor, and Days Inns of America, with ADA violations.

When I tracked down John L. Wodatch, chief of the Justice Department's disability rights section, to find out why the Hauks had been singled out, he claimed that under the law he had no choice but to take action. "The Hauks' architect and contractor, as well as Days Inns of America, reviewed the plans for their hotel, but did not alert them to potential ADA problems." Presumably, Wodatch was saying the Hauks had no option except to sue everyone who had given them advice. Yet, as I discovered, the Justice Department did reach settlements for modifications with three other motels without levying fines or civil penalties.

So why single out this couple of modest means in South Dakota? The Justice Department needed at least one major victory, a trophy scalp, to flaunt as a warning to other motel and hotel owners. The resulting publicity in *Reader's Digest*, however, clearly showed the unfairness of the Justice Department's demands on the couple, and this apparently had the effect of forcing the agency to retreat from its insensitive position.

On June 5, 1997, the parties reached a settlement. The Hauks were required to remake the sidewalks, modify bathtubs, repaint parking spaces, and other alterations costing $20,000. The lawsuit had cost them an additional $10,000 in attorney's fees, just a fraction of the actual cost because the Hauks' lawyer was Karla's sister, who provided much of the work for free.

"The Justice Department turned us into a test case to prove a point," Karla told me, "even if it almost drove us out of business." Meanwhile, during the five-year period after settlement of their case, they rented out their handicapped rooms to people with disabilities only eight times.

The Denver Entrepreneur

Within a week of opening The Barolo Grill, an upscale Italian restaurant in Denver, owner Blair Taylor received a phone call from an attorney with the U.S. Justice Department in Washington, D.C. "We have a complaint that your restaurant is in noncompliance with the Americans With Disabilities Act," said the civil rights division attorney.

Forty-year-old Taylor had received no complaints from patrons, nor did he even have any idea what compliance with the ADA entailed. His restaurant had only been open a week and he thought the complaint must have been some kind of mistake. He had enough problems working eighteen-hour days overseeing his new business, so he asked his personal attorney to look into the matter.

Enacted by Congress in 1990, and intended to ensure that disabled persons had access to public facilities, the ADA required, among other things, that any public facility undergoing renovation "make alterations in such a manner that, to the maximum extent feasible, the altered portions are readily accessible to and usable by individuals with disabilities." Taylor had renovated the building he bought to accommodate his new restaurant. As a result, he unwittingly fell under these guidelines.

A second letter to Taylor from the Justice Department in January 1993 accused him of placing eight of the restaurant's twenty-four tables on an eighteen-inch elevated platform without a wheelchair ramp, and failing to install a ramp in front of the building from the sidewalk up a seven-inch step to the doorway. Two-thirds of Taylor's tables were wheelchair accessible and he had two valet attendants in front at all times to assist patrons through the entrance, but he agreed anyway to build the wheelchair ramp in the spring, once the snow had melted enough to pour concrete.

On April 2, ten minutes before the restaurant opened for dinner, a van pulled up in front and four wheelchair demonstrators rolled themselves out carrying protest signs. They belonged to Atlantis/ ADAPT, a lobby and advocacy group for the disabled. A photographer they brought along snapped pictures as the protestors blocked the restaurant's entrance and waved signs reading: "Down On Barolo" and "Blair Sucks." When Taylor tried to reason with them, it quickly became apparent the protest had been inspired by, if not coordinated by, the U.S. Justice Department. One protestor repeated to Taylor the name of the attorney at the Justice Department who had written him the letters. "You promised her you would get us a ramp," the protestor shouted.

"You will have a wheelchair ramp," Taylor replied. "I'm pouring the concrete next week."

As promised, Taylor personally built the ramp, but he had to do so without obtaining a city permit because it would have taken up to four months for approval. The ramp he constructed would end up being used by just two wheelchairs out of 3,000 diners each month. He also began planning an interior remodeling effort to erect another ramp and create bathrooms that would meet all ADA specifications for the disabled.

In June a city building inspector visited Taylor and decreed that Barolo Grill had to obtain city permits for the entire structure rather than just the areas that would be renovated. Meanwhile, Barolo was "red-tagged" by this inspector, which amounted to a cease and desist order that prevented Taylor from undertaking any ADA-mandated work until the necessary local permits were issued. In a further escalation of this nightmare, an architect advised Taylor that the permits would require a series of separate time-consuming studies for electrical systems, the rooftop, wastewater, and plumbing.

After months of hearings before zoning and variance boards, Taylor finally got his permits in February 1994. By this time, however, the Justice Department was threatening to file suit against him for being out of compliance with the ADA. He started construction to add handrails on the entrance ramp, create an interior ramp, wheelchair-friendly bathrooms, and a new electrical system to incorporate strobelight fire alarms for the hearing impaired. He completed construction by April 1, yet ten days later he was served with a federal lawsuit alleging noncompliance with the ADA.

The lawsuit detailed a mind-numbing list of actions Taylor had to undertake to bring Barolo into "full" compliance with the law. He was ordered to rebuild the front wheelchair ramp because its handrail was not precisely one-and-a-half inches from the window glass. He had to replace doorknobs with narrow gripping surfaces, rebuild the interior ramp, and make a wine storage room in the rear of the restaurant accessible to wheelchairs by widening the door and erecting still another ramp. Signs identifying bathrooms had to be in Braille, as did exit signs. Bathroom walls had to be extended three inches closer to the toilets so that the centerline of the toilets was precisely eighteen inches to the wall.

As a further insult, the Justice Department demanded that Taylor pay a $50,000 fine, and monetary damages to persons in wheelchairs "denied access to the Barolo Grill's services to compensate them for injuries resulting from its discrimination." Taylor had never denied entrance to anyone who was disabled. Then he remembered the four protestors. None of them had ever asked to dine at Barolo, yet it was those four persons the Justice Department wanted Taylor to compensate. He was being forced to reward them for professional picketing!

Throughout the remainder of 1994 Taylor endured new rounds of indignities and annoyances. Justice Department attorneys subpoenaed his personal and business tax returns back to 1980, and depositions were taken from all of his employees and contractors. Unable to afford legal counsel anymore, Taylor tried to obtain a bank loan, but no bank would loan him money because of the federal lawsuit. No longer able to afford an apartment of his own, Taylor had to move in with a friend. Only the intervention of Taylor's father, who put the family home up for collateral on a loan to pay legal bills, saved Taylor from bankruptcy.

In November 1994 the case went into settlement before a federal judge. Financially exhausted, Taylor agreed to take any steps necessary to finally satisfy the Justice Department's interpretation of the ADA. He had to produce restaurant menus in Braille, and an employee manual on how to serve the disabled, and he was ordered to host a one-day "ADA awareness seminar" for Denver restaurant owners. He also had to pay the four protestors $1,500 each for the "humiliation" they suffered while picketing his restaurant.

Altogether, Taylor ended up spending more than $100,000 on fines, legal bills, and construction, to conform with ADA guidelines. "Why me?" Taylor asked when I visited him at his restaurant. "Because the Justice Department needed a scalp for the ADA that it could hold up and threaten other restaurant owners with. I became their publicity statement."

In the Name of Equal Employment

The Ohio Market Owner

As Russell Vernon sat in the office of his West Point Market in Akron, Ohio, reading the daily mail, a letter from the U.S. Equal Employment Opportunity Commission in Washington, D.C., grabbed his attention. The one-page letter from the commissioner's office accused Vernon of discriminating against blacks in his hiring practices.

Vernon, a tall, lanky mild-mannered man who wears bowties and always speaks in courteous tones, felt his shock rapidly turn to indignation. "This can't be," he erupted, "It's got to be a mistake. No one has ever complained about us."

Founded in 1936 by Vernon's father and two associates, West Point had grown into a neighborhood specialty food store with a reputation for high quality. It employed more than one hundred persons and never in Vernon's memory, certainly not since he became president in 1978, had any allegation of discrimination been made by an employee or prospective employee.

The investigation of "pattern and practice" discrimination, as the charge against West Point was called, allegedly involved an examination of 1,500 employment applications of successful and unsuccessful applicants between July 1, 1991 and May 11, 1994. Even though West Point's applications did not identify job applicants by race, the EEOC indicated that it would determine whether discrimination existed by interviewing "former and present employees, and rejected applicants," which presumably would reveal whether a pattern existed showing discriminatory practices.

By January 26, 1995, the EEOC had concluded, based on this survey, that West Point violated Title VII of the Civil Rights Act of 1964 by "engaging in recruitment practices which discriminate against blacks; by failing to hire blacks into entry-level positions; and failing to maintain proper records on its employment process." According to the EEOC, West Point had hired 236 entry-level service workers from 1991 to 1994, of whom 22 (9 percent) were African-American, compared to a black application rate of 19 percent. "This result is statistically significant," wrote EEOC executive officer Frances Hart, and supposedly showed a pattern of discrimination.

What disturbed Vernon most about the EEOC's verdict was its charge that West Point "has a reputation in the community for racial bias." This accusation, originating with an unidentified EEOC source, reinforced his determination to fight the charges. "They've attacked our reputation," he told family and friends, "That breaks my heart."

Under the EEOC's proposed settlement, West Point would have to buy full-page recruitment ads aimed solely at blacks, impose a 33 percent minority hiring quota, and pay nearly $100,000 to twenty-four African-Americans the EEOC singled out as having been denied employment at West Point. The law firm that Vernon hired had advised him to settle on the EEOC's terms and "give them whatever they want," because the agency rarely lost these sorts of cases. Vernon refused and hired a new team of lawyers.

Meanwhile, news of these EEOC charges baffled and outraged leaders of Akron's African-American community, and they began to rally to West Point's defense. An August 1995 petition signed by thirty-six black community leaders, including the entire board of Akron's NAACP branch, stated: "We have never seen or heard of any unfair practices at West Point. We will stand by them all the way." That petition effectively exposed the EEOC's contention that West Point had a reputation for racial bias as a lie.

NAACP President Ophelia Averitt, whose son had been a West Point employee, was even more adamant in the market's defense. "I am appalled that the EEOC takes these charges seriously. I have never had problems of any kind with their hiring practices," she told me in an interview. Neither Averitt nor any other NAACP board member had been contacted during the EEOC's investigation, which prompted Averitt to question the agency's motives. "They must have some kind of enforcement quota or something to meet," she speculated to me.

To refute the EEOC's statistical claims of bias, Vernon hired a statistician to analyze the 1,500 employment applications for evidence of hiring bias. This study found that West Point had hired African-Americans at the rates expected for its location and labor pool needs, and at the same rate as other area food retailers, none of which had ever been targeted by the EEOC.

Vernon also took his case of having been unfairly singled out to the Ohio media. After months of negotiations, during which several statewide officeholders wrote to the EEOC on Vernon's behalf, the two sides reached a conciliation agreement in October 1996. This time, to end the expensive legal battle, Vernon accepted the more lenient terms. Under the agreement West Point would invite the twenty-four applicants cited in the EEOC's original decision to reapply for positions. For any of the twenty-four who stayed on the job for a full year, West Point would give them a $1,000 scholarship to the academic institution of their choice.

Just one of the twenty-four persons ever reapplied, and she worked less than a year. Even more damning, West Point's director of Human Resources, Terri Freiman, discovered that one of the persons cited in the EEOC complaint was a white woman who had previously worked at West Point for several weeks. That cast a longer and darker shadow on the thoroughness of the EEOC's "investigation."

After spending $67,000 on legal fees to defend his reputation, Vernon believes he learned a valuable lesson that can be shared with other small-business owners. "Logic and reason don't enter into dealing with federal regulatory agencies," he declared, "The EEOC used poor research methods and they refused to admit they were wrong. That kind of arrogance is dangerous. The only thing that saved me was my persistence in doing what I thought was right, and making my case to the local media, which helped rally public opinion against the EEOC."

The Chicago Restaurateur

Ever since Hans Morsbach opened the first of his four Chicago restaurants in 1963, he had prided himself on employing a diverse workforce because he felt being a good employer should be as important as making a profit. Born in Germany in 1932, he had emigrated to the U.S. and received an MBA from the University of Chicago, and it was around this campus that he established his restaurants that attracted a mostly student clientele. So when an investigator for the U.S. Equal Employment Opportunity Commission visited one of his restaurants in January 1994, requesting copies of personnel files,

Morsbach thought it was routine and paid little attention. After all, he told himself, three-fourths of the restaurant staff were minorities and women.

Three months later Morsbach got the shock of his life when the same EEOC investigator informed him that he was being formally charged with discriminatory hiring practices. Morsbach, sixty-one years old, stood accused of violating the Age Discrimination in Employment Act, a 1967 federal law banning discrimination against people over the age of forty.

"What is the evidence against me?" Morsbach demanded to know in a meeting with an EEOC supervisor in Chicago.

"We've already established guilt," replied the supervisor, "Now let's talk about remedies."

Morsbach was ordered to hire four persons over the age of forty—to be selected by the EEOC—and give them seven months backpay and benefits amounting to many thousands of dollars. Not only that, he had to post signs in his four restaurants admitting his guilt and promising never to discriminate again. These demands, said the EEOC supervisor, were "non-negotiable." How did these charges originate? Morsbach wondered. A few days later a certified letter arrived with the answer. "The finding is based in large part on a notice placed with an employment agency seeking 'wts,' described as 'young bub.'" Thereafter, according to the EEOC, one of Morsbach's restaurant managers, aged forty-seven, had hired four persons under the age of forty to wait tables.

Morsbach read the EEOC letter in disbelief. "What is a 'bub'?" he asked. He had never heard the expression before and he could not find it in the dictionary. Could it perhaps have been slang for "bubbly"? As for "wts," which presumably meant waitresses, Morsbach could only plead ignorance. He had not placed any notice using such language with any employment agencies.

As Morsbach would eventually learn, the complaint against him arose from an unrelated investigation. An EEOC investigator, while looking through the records of an employment agency, came across a twelve-word file card concerning a Morsbach restaurant on which someone had written the "wts" and "young bub" references. There was absolutely no evidence that Morsbach or any of his employees had ever used the slang in dealing with the agency, yet this had become the "evidence" the EEOC used to decide his guilt.

Rather than agree to the EEOC "remedy," Morsbach decided to fight the charge. "I've done nothing wrong and I have a clear conscience," he told his wife. Lawyer friends urged Morsbach to settle the complaint on EEOC terms. "You are out of your mind to fight this," one attorney warned him, "It'll cost you dearly."

Chicago's EEOC office, with thirty-two investigators and fourteen attorneys, had developed a gunslinger's reputation as an aggressive filer of lawsuits. Area businesses had been forced to pay millions of dollars in fines and legal fees, and no one wanted to be in the EEOC's gun sights for any length of time, so settlements usually happened quickly.

Enraged by the arrogance of EEOC bureaucrats, Morsbach took his case to columnist Mike Royko of the *Chicago Tribune*. In a series of blistering columns, Royko revealed how the EEOC had used frivolous cases like the one against Morsbach to terrorize small entrepreneurs and extort money from them throughout the Chicago area.

An examination of the Chicago EEOC office by *Crain's Small Business* magazine came to a similar conclusion: "Laws intended to ensure equality in the workplace often become bludgeons used to extract cash settlements and other concessions from small employers who believe their employment practices to be fair and unbiased. Owners of businesses sued by the EEOC tell strikingly similar stories of investigators who seem to presume an employer is guilty, and an investigative process that affords the employer scant opportunity to present a defense."

Morsbach met with EEOC district director John P. Rowe, at Rowe's request, on August 3, 1994. When Morsbach walked into Rowe's office he found the Royko columns laid out on Rowe's desk, which Rowe used to accuse Morsbach of flouting the EEOC's authority. Replied Morsbach, "Sir, the only thing I would accept from you is a letter of apology."

Two months later Rowe informed Morsbach that his case had been referred to Washington, D.C., where "the question of what further action is to be taken" would be decided by the EEOC commissioners, who turned about 70 percent of such referrals into lawsuits. In another ominous development for Morsbach during March 1995, Rowe himself moved to Washington to become acting general counsel for the agency.

Cooler heads apparently prevailed in Washington, because Morsbach was never prosecuted. Years later, as he reflected on the entire incident, his anger still simmered. "I'd be the first to support laws against discrimination. But the EEOC just wants notches on their gun. They're an agency out of control."

5

Mugged by
HEALTH AND SAFETY
REGULATIONS

WHEN THE FEDERAL GOVERNMENT tried to put Gertrude Spindler out of the snack bar baking business in early 2002, it did so on the pretext of protecting public health and safety from an illegal drug. The sixty-year-old San Diego entrepreneur was using hempnuts, one of nature's best sources of essential fatty acids, as a staple in the health bars she provided distributors in six states.

Hempnuts come from hemp, an industrial plant whose fiber is used to make rope, clothing, and paper, and whose oil can be found widely sold in body lotions and cosmetics. While hemp is related to marijuana, its THC content, the psychoactive chemical found in marijuana, is so negligible that it can be considered undetectable. Certainly it is well below any level that would produce a high. Yet, the U.S. Drug Enforcement Administration ruled that Spindler's health bars, along with the chips, pretzels, waffles, granola, and a range of other food products made by twenty companies, must be banned under the Controlled Substances Act for containing even one trace molecule of THC.

The logic used to justify this ruling defies common sense. No true zero of any chemical exists in nature. Even the EPA allows trace levels of arsenic in drinking water, and the FDA accepts trace levels of alcohol in orange juice. DEA's agenda in seeking to ban edible hemp products, rather than being rooted in any legitimate public health and safety concern, was based on a premise of drug warrior ideology—that the war itself justifies using any means necessary to eradicate the threat.

Regulatory muggings that occur in the name of public health and safety often come promoting hidden agendas. Take the Occupational Safety and Health Administration and its minefield of rules and regulations. Anyone—a business competitor, a disgruntled former employee—can file an anonymous complaint with OSHA against a business and trigger an investigation that can lead to an endless and costly nightmare, even if the original charge proves baseless. At the local level, health and safety regulations routinely become a tool for the exercise of monopoly power, a trend demonstrated more thoroughly in Chapter 6, as licensing standards needlessly restrict entry into many professions and limit competition to the detriment of both consumers and aspiring entrepreneurs.

The Maine Fish Processor

For nearly a century the McCurdy Fish Company had been an employment mainstay in the village of Lubec, Maine, processing smoked and salted herring caught by local fishermen. Ownership had passed down from grandfather to father and then to son John, who was sixty-four years old when the problems began. Herring smokehouses had been a foundation of Lubec's economy since 1797—at one point in the nineteenth century thirty were in operation—but by 1975 America's eating habits had changed and McCurdy's was the last commercial smoked herring processor in the nation.

At least once a year, the U.S. Food and Drug Administration inspected McCurdy Fish Company's facilities, and never in the company's history had it ever been cited for a serious violation of health and safety regulations. In May 1990, just a few weeks before the fish season would begin, an FDA official visited John McCurdy and handed him a FDA Policy Guide regulation labeled 7108.17.

Three outbreaks of botulism in 1981, 1985, and 1987, producing a total of eleven illnesses in New York City, had been traced to Great Lakes Whitefish which had been processed by layering ungutted fish in salt and then air-drying it. Acting on the assumption that the process was a life-threatening acute health hazard, the FDA banned the distribution of any fish that was salt-cured and air-dried prior to being gutted.

As McCurdy read the regulation he knew immediately that it would put him out of business. His smoked herring had been processed this way by hand for eighty-eight years. To comply with the regulation he would have to purchase gutting machines and refrigerated salting tanks costing more than $200,000. That sum was far out of reach for a company with just twenty employees.

Then the timing of the two-page regulation captured McCurdy's attention and the implications baffled him. The regulation was dated October 27, 1988, a full nineteen months earlier. If he was producing such a "life-threatening acute health hazard," in FDA terminology, why had the agency waited nearly two years to inform him and "protect" the public? The FDA investigator shrugged. "Possibly because you're such a small processor."

With his economic future hanging in the balance, McCurdy phoned FDA officials in Washington, D.C., to explain how there could be no possible comparison between the whitefish targeted by the agency and the herring he processed. Whitefish was larger and caught from freshwaters, while herring was an ocean saltwater species whose natural saltiness, combined with McCurdy's salting process, prevented the growth of botulism spores. Besides that, as the FDA conceded, not a single case of botulism had ever been reported in sea herring.

Totally unmoved by McCurdy's logic or his pleas for understanding, an FDA official restated his agency's position. If McCurdy tried to distribute any of the most recent herring catch he had already contracted for, the FDA would seize the fish and take legal action against him. Faced with bankruptcy, McCurdy appealed to then-U.S. Senator William Cohen of Maine, who contacted the FDA and succeeded in securing a temporary stay of execution until that season's catch had been processed.

Over the next four months FDA inspectors made eight unannounced visits to McCurdy's plant, spending two and three days each time monitoring his processing methods. No evidence of contamination was found. But it would be McCurdy's last season because the FDA refused even to consider an exception to its blanket ruling.

The day McCurdy hung a large "For Sale" sign on the side of his processing plant was the saddest day of his life. He had to say goodbye to his twenty employees, who were his friends and neighbors. Many of them, like him, had grown up working in the plant.

Years later McCurdy remained understandably hurt and angry about his forced retirement. Those feelings are only compounded by the continued sale in the U.S. of Canadian herring using the exact process the FDA outlawed for American producers. FDA officials told me they had no way of certifying which processing methods are used by Canadian suppliers. The McCurdy mugging illustrates the FDA's insensitivity toward the realities of operating a small business, and the one-size-fits-all nature of its ruling in this case shows how inflexible regulatory agencies can inflict an economic toll far beyond any reasonable justification for its actions.

The Virginia Dry Cleaner

Three employees called in sick on December 19, 1991, the busiest week of the year at Wayside Cleaners in Portsmouth, Virginia. Co-owner Bill Griggs was frantically trying to write payroll checks while filling in for his missing workers when an inspector for the Virginia Department of Labor and Industry, the state agency that enforces regulations for the U.S. Occupational Safety and Health Administration (OSHA), marched into his office.

She flashed her badge and announced, "I'm here to inspect you." She asked to see a long list of Wayside's records, including labor, safety, and hazardous waste logs. In a daze the forty-year-old Griggs walked to the rear of the building and alerted his seventy-year-old father, Joe. Both men were perplexed. In thirty-five years of doing business they had never heard of a single complaint against them. Why now?

An OSHA inspection can be initiated by a customer, a disgruntled employee, a competitor, just about anyone, and inspectors will not reveal how the complaint originated. Once underway, an OSHA investigation is open-ended in both the scope and the time devoted to it.

For three full days the OSHA inspector, armed with a 745-page manual of fine-print regulations, scrutinized every square foot of Wayside looking for violations. Either Bill or his father had to be available at all times to answer her seemingly endless questions. Bill found many of the manual's regulations incomprehensible. He suspected that such regulatory complexity would make a few technical violations unavoidable. "She'll find something somewhere wrong," he warned his father, "because every day our employees change something and we may not catch it immediately."

Bill was shocked speechless when at the end of the three days the inspector handed him a list of thirty "serious" violations, making him liable for over $39,000 in fines. As he scanned the list Bill shook his head in disbelief. Of Wayside's 100 electrical outlets, one was found to have reversed polarity. Did that single mistake by a licensed electrician warrant a $750 fine?

Other so-called serious violations seemed merely innocuous. Though Griggs had exit signs hanging over every door, one citation said he failed to post exit maps throughout the small building so that. employees could plan an escape in an emergency. "As if they can't remember how they walk in the building every morning," Bill noted dryly.

Several citations were simply wrong. Wayside was accused of permitting smoking in flammable liquid storage areas. Yet it was Wayside's policy that employees could smoke only in an enclosed bathroom separated from the work area by a cement wall.

To correct other violations would have put Griggs in conflict with local ordinances. For instance, OSHA cited him for locating electrical equipment within twenty feet of paint spray booths. Yet the room had been specifically configured to satisfy the building code, and to separate the electrical equipment from paint booths by more than twenty feet would have required expanding the building in violation of local zoning.

Meanwhile, the heavy hand of a second regulatory agency descended on Wayside Cleaners. Air quality standards enacted in September 1993 by the Environmental Protection Agency—regulating solvents used in the cleaning process—meant Griggs would have to spend $300,000 on emissions control machinery and plant renovation. Even if Griggs succeeded in obtaining a zoning exemption to expand his plant, he would be unable to secure a loan to cover his costs. The regulatory burdens faced by dry cleaners—plus the threat of litigation under the federal Superfund Act—had frightened most banks away from making loans to the industry.

To comply with the EPA, Griggs was forced to close the leather and suede cleaning part of his business in August 1994, since it was the primary target of the emissions regulation. That decision cost Wayside one-third of its cleaning business revenue and resulted in the firing of fifteen employees, one-third of its workforce.

On the OSHA front, it took Griggs two years to resolve all of the compliance issues raised in just one inspection. Wayside emerged from the process financially battered, but still in business thanks to a loyal clientele. Other dry cleaners are not so fortunate. The typical establishment is family-owned, employing five persons, with an average profit of $10,000 a year, according to statistics compiled by a trade group representing the dry cleaning industry. Just one nit-picking OSHA inspector can mean the difference between survival and ruin.

The Illinois Bakery Owner

Judy Hooper was doing paperwork in her Evanston, Illinois, bakery on the morning that an employee of the Occupational Safety and Health Administration showed up to conduct an unannounced inspection of her facilities. "I have a complaint from one of your employees," said the inspector, "If you don't want to proceed with this inspection, you may request that we obtain a warrant."

"No need for that," replied Hooper, who had no reason not to cooperate, "What do you want to see?"

The inspector pulled out the complaint listing four alleged violations of OSHA regulations. In the first allegation, kitchen heat in Judy's Bakery supposedly exceeded 120 degrees, causing employees to experience tremors, dizziness, and incoherent thoughts. As the thirty-three-year-old Hooper watched, the inspector took temperature readings in the kitchen. All readings were in the mid-80s, well within OSHA guidelines. Nor did any kitchen employee complain to the inspector of heat-exhaustion symptoms.

One by one the inspector examined and then dismissed the other complaints, but she continued looking around and photographing parts of the bakery. It was clear that she had initiated an open-ended investigation. After three hours the inspector announced to Hooper, "If there are any problems, you'll hear from us."

One month later a letter came from OSHA area director Ronald McCann. As Hooper read it her jaw dropped open. The bakery was being fined $13,000 for seven violations of OSHA regulations, only one of which was even remotely connected to the original complaint. Among the fines assessed against her: $2,500 for slippery stairs leading to the basement; $2,500 for not having written fire-prevention and emergency action plans, despite having four clearly marked fire exits; and $2,500 for failing to have a "hazard communication program" training employees to protect themselves against hazardous chemicals, even though the only chemicals used in the bakery were common household bleach and dishwashing liquids.

Judy and her husband Bill fixed all of the alleged problems within two days of receiving the list of complaints. They then attended a settlement hearing with McCann and the inspector, thinking their prompt action might be rewarded with some degree of leniency. Instead, McCann's only compromise was to make $7,550 of the fines payable in the form of expenditures on health and safety programs for bakery employees. The remaining $5,450 had to be paid immediately and directly to the U.S. Department of the Treasury.

After the Hoopers paid their fines, under protest, Judy wrote to members of Congress arguing that OSHA's open-ended investigations, initiated by mere rumor or innuendo, were an unnecessary and onerous burden on small-business owners. "It's not worth it to work eighteen-hour days, seven days a week only to be treated this way by our own government," she declared.

The North Carolina Cake Maker

When it came to the quality of her pound cakes and peach cobblers, few bakers in Charlotte, North Carolina, could rival what Thelma Connell produced in the kitchen of her home. After retiring from her job as a dental assistant, Connell knew she had to supplement her modest Social Security benefits with extra income. So she decided to sell her delicious baked goods at the nearby Charlotte Regional Farmers Market.

Thinking that such sales might, at the most, require that her kitchen be inspected, Connell contacted the local health department. But an employee there suggested that she should phone the county zoning board. She did call and an employee of the board informed Connell that her house was in an area zoned for residential use only.

"I know that," replied Connell, I've lived here since 1954. All I want to do is sell a few cakes and pies every once in a while."

Sorry, she was told, but residential zoning means you cannot publicly sell what you make in your home. Under the zoning regulations anything baked at home, or any handicrafts created there, constituted a business, and a person could only operate a business—no matter how small or irregular—in areas zoned specifically for business or industrial use. If she violated the zoning ordinance, she was subject to fines.

The maddening and arbitrary nature of this ordinance quickly made Connell aware of how even the most innocuous fundraising efforts in the city were technically illegal. Cakes and pies that she and other members of her church group made for church fundraisers were being sold illegally, as were handicrafts that civic group members were producing in their homes for public sale to support charitable causes.

Fuming about this limitation of her economic options, Connell did her own inspection of the local Farmer's Market and found a wide range of baked goods for sale, all prepared in people's homes. These people lived outside of the county, where the ordinance did not apply. The unfairness of this situation still grates on Connell and other would-be entrepreneurs.

"It's silly that I can sell my baked goods and handicrafts across the county line, or in neighboring South Carolina, but I can't sell in my own county where I pay taxes," Connell complained to me when I visited her in Charlotte during 1997. "I don't want a full-time business. I don't have any retirement benefits other than Social Security. I really need the extra income. What is someone like me to do?"

6

Mugged by
MONOPOLY POWER

COUNTLESS CONFUSING REGULATIONS and ordinances restricting economic activity have been put in place by city, county, and state governments, usually on the pretext of protecting public health and safety. An extensive study of these regulatory barriers, conducted by the Institute for Justice in 1996, examined the hardships faced by low-income entrepreneurs in seven cities—Charlotte, San Diego, New York, San Antonio, Baltimore, and Detroit.

Do you want to repair VCRs, shovel snow, or usher at a wrestling match? You need a license to do so in New York City, which maintains an official directory with seventy-three pages of occupations that require certification. Anyone practicing without certification is subject to prosecution. In San Antonio cutting hair in the home is prohibited. Baltimore will not allow newsstands on city sidewalks. Detroit refuses to allow permit vendors to sell any hot food except hot dogs and sausages. You can sell razor blades but not books on the sidewalks of New Orleans. The list of these absurd restrictions on making an honest income stretches on endlessly. The Institute for Justice's study found three main categories of barriers to entrepreneurs: Public monopolies, especially in mass transit and trash collection, where government prohibits private competition; ceilings on permits for certain occupations; and occupational licensing standards that bear no relationship to legitimate public health and safety concerns.

"There are thousands of such laws and restrictions on economic opportunity cluttering the statute books of almost every major jurisdiction in the nation," concluded Chip Mellor, president and cofounder of the Institute for Justice, "Few of these regulations are fair or worthwhile. They are institutionalized impediments to low-income and fixed-income persons climbing up the lower rungs of opportunity, and are designed to insulate monopolies from healthy competition that would lower costs to consumers."

Most Americans take for granted a few basic assumptions about how our free enterprise system should work. One, that each individual should be free to pursue the livelihood of his or her choice. Two, this freedom of competition generally benefits both businesses and consumers. Three, the government's role, if it has any at all to play, should be one of facilitating this competition rather than taking sides to unfairly advantage any single competitor. In practice, however, as you will see from the following examples, financial and political power all too often translates into monopoly privilege.

The San Diego Hair Braiders

When two inspectors for the California Board of Barbering and Cosmetology showed up unannounced at The Braiderie, a San Diego, California, hair braiding salon, the alarmed receptionist immediately phoned Ali Rasheed, one of the salon's three owners. Rasheed told her to put one of the inspectors on the phone.

"What is going on?" asked Rasheed.

"What you are doing is covered under the cosmetology law," said the inspector, referring to the salon's specialized technique of braiding hair naturally without chemicals.

"No license is required for braiding," Rasheed objected, "Braiding is not even taught in cosmetology school."

Rasheed had researched the law and knew that it made no mention of hairbraiding, nor did any cosmetology school in the state teach the African hairstyling techniques of braiding, cornrowing, twisting, and locking hair. It made no sense to him that his seven African-American employees would need nine months of cosmetology school—at a cost of up to $7,000 each—to obtain a license for a range of procedures that his salon had never provided its customers.

Rasheed and his two partners, his wife Assiyah, and Marguerite Sylva, opened The Braiderie in 1992, with investments of their life savings. They had never cut, curled or straightened hair, or used chemicals. Only braiding was offered, and that amounted to a professionalizing of techniques that had previously been performed informally within people's homes. The braiders they hired were immigrants from Senegal and Guinea who had no other marketable skills.

None of this information swayed the inspectors, who defined the cosmetology licensing law as being broad enough to encompass hairbraiding even though it was not specifically described in the law. They fined the salon $200 for "aiding and abetting" the unlicensed practice of hairbraiding. Unless you get licensed, Rasheed was warned, we will shut you down.

Faced with the loss of his livelihood, Rasheed, a fifty-four-year-old U.S. Navy veteran, conferred with his two partners about what to do. "We can't just let them run over us like this," he declared, "They're trying to rob us of our ability to make a living." They all agreed they had to fight back, so they filed an administrative appeal of the board's decision, and in early in 1997, thanks to intervention by the Institute for Justice, they became plaintiffs in a federal lawsuit challenging California's cosmetology law. It was being pursued on behalf of Dr. JoAnne Cornwell, the chairwoman of the African-Studies Department at San Diego State University, who had trademarked a hairstyling technique called "sister-locks."

"We don't object to standards for public health and safety," Rasheed explained in my interview with him, "But these licenses aren't about that. This is about government overregulation and control."

All fifty states require licenses for anyone working with hair, and typically the state and city boards of cosmetology, which set the profession's licensing standards, are composed of licensed salon owners. Their temptation is always to exceed legitimate health and safety concerns and use the regulations they create to limit competition. The result is discrimination "against outsiders, latecomers and the resourceless," in the words of George Mason University economist Walter Williams.

It is ironic that the licensing laws harassing hair braiders today were conceived in the 1930s by hairdressers to break an economic stranglehold over their profession then held by barbers. Previous occupational licensing laws had given barbers and cosmeticians (who performed skin care and some haircutting) a monopoly over all types of hair treatment, and in some states hairdressers were actually arrested, fined, and jailed, for violating these regulations.

While the regulations that subsequently evolved vary from state to state, they rarely have any relation to public health and safety needs. In New York, for example, hair braiders have been required to take 900 hours of cosmetology classes to obtain a license, compared to 116 hours of training for emergency medical technicians, and just 47 hours for security guards authorized to use deadly force. Ohio's regulations exceeded even this level of absurdity. To braid someone else's hair in that state you needed 1,500 hours of cosmetology school, more than twice the number of hours of training as required of a paramedic engaged in saving other people's lives. As

Institute for Justice attorney Dana Berliner pointed out, "In Ohio I could become qualified to run a restaurant, carry a gun, be a volunteer fire fighter, care for children, protect the public as a police officer, and respond to emergencies as a paramedic, all in less time than it would take to get a license to braid hair."

Until 1992 hair braiders in Washington, D.C., were required to take 1,500 hours of cosmetology classes-at up to $5,000 per student-and pass a written exam to receive a license. In that year the owners of a braiding salon, Cornrows & Co., aided by Institute for Justice co-founder Clint Bolick, filed suit in federal court challenging the regulation and $1,000 in fines that had been levied against the salon's owners. In response to a public outcry once the lawsuit and its circumstances were publicized, the District of Columbia City Council amended the law in 1993 to exempt hair braiders from cosmetology licensing.

A San Diego federal judge handed California hair braiders and the Institute a huge victory in August 1999, ruling that the state's cosmetology regulations "failed to pass constitutional muster" under the due process and equal protection clauses of the Fourteenth Amendment. In his twenty-six-page opinion Judge Rudi Brewster asked, "How do you license what you do not teach? How do you teach what you do not know?" The judge agreed that these arbitrary regulations cut the bottom rungs off the economic ladder for many women trying to escape welfare, and did so in a way that preserved monopoly privileges for a select few.

The Tennessee Casket Seller

On a visit to New York City in June 1997, the Reverend Nathaniel Craigmiles, a church pastor from Chattanooga, Tennessee, happened to walk past a funeral casket store and noticed a steel casket with an $800 price tag. "Hey, look at this!" Craigmiles exclaimed to his wife,

"This is the same exact casket we paid $3,200 for back in Chattanooga to bury your grandmother in."

Concerned that his family might have been cheated by someone taking advantage of their grief, Craigmiles returned to Chattanooga and began researching funeral home costs. He was amazed to discover a vast difference in wholesale and retail prices of caskets and burial urns. The steel casket Craigmiles buried his wife's grandmother in, for example, could be purchased wholesale for less than $500, but funeral homes were selling it for nearly seven times that amount.

Craigmile's church congregation on the south side of Chattanooga came from neighborhoods that struggled with poverty and crime. For them, even more than most American families, a funeral—which costs $8,000, on average—is the third largest investment they will make in their lives after purchases of a home and a vehicle. "Why don't we provide our people with low-cost caskets?" Craigmiles, fifty-two years old, proposed to a member of his congregation, seventy-five-year-old Tommy Wilson, who had spent much of his life working as a nightshift ambulance driver for local funeral homes.

These two men formed a storefront business, Craigmiles Wilson Casket Supply, and obtained business licenses from the city and county. From their savings they spent $6,200 to purchase eleven caskets, and on March 1, 1999, they opened for business offering caskets at prices half that charged by area funeral homes.

Four months later Craigmiles received a letter from Arthur Giles, executive director of the Board of Funeral Directors and Embalmers, a state agency in Nashville with oversight of the funeral industry. "You must immediately cease and desist all sales of caskets," read the notice, threatening them with prosecution, "Neither you nor Mr. Wilson hold current and valid funeral director licenses."

Under Tennessee law, in order to sell caskets a person must attend a state approved funeral directing school for one year, at a cost of about $8,000, with coursework that included the preparation of bodies for burial. After graduation an applicant must pass an examination for a funeral director's license.

"People aren't required to buy a car from a mechanic," Craigmiles reasoned in response, "So why should people be forced to buy overpriced caskets from funeral homes?"

Officials with the Board of Funeral Directors and Embalmers declined to answer this question. Instead they claimed that only "qualified" people should sell caskets because "a defective casket, once buried, could harm the environment and endanger public health." The state claimed it needed regulatory control to protect consumers. But as Craigmiles rightfully countered, there is no public health issue here. After all, he purchased his caskets from the same manufacturers as did licensed funeral homes-the only difference between his caskets and funeral home caskets was the price charged consumers. Not only that, but thirty-eight states do not require caskets to be sold by licensed funeral directors, and none of those thirty-eight have reported any problems with defective caskets endangering public health.

With legal help from the Institute for Justice, Craigmiles and Wilson took the state's Funeral Board to federal court. Their lawsuit argued that Tennessee's funeral laws violate due process and equal-protection guarantees in the Fourteenth Amendment to the Constitution. "Six of the seven members of the funeral board are funeral home directors," noted Chip Mellor, the Institute's president, "They have a vested interest in protecting the funeral industry from competition. By limiting competition, funeral directors can greatly overcharge consumers."

After a two-day trial in which expert testimony was presented, a U.S. district court judge sided with Craigmiles that the Tennessee law did violate the Fourteenth Amendment. State funeral directors appealed this ruling to the U.S. Court of Appeals for the Sixth Circuit. Meanwhile, the Institute for Justice filed a federal lawsuit against

Oklahoma for protecting its licensed funeral homes from competition. Eleven other states maintain similar anti-competitive laws protecting the funeral industry.

Driven Out of Businesss...Literally

The New York Van Drivers

As he awaited his appearance before the transportation committee of the New York City Council, Vincent Cummins felt elated at a dream come true. For five years he had navigated a complex regulatory maze, spending $40,000 of his life savings on legal and other fees, to obtain license approval for a van service in Brooklyn that would create eighty new jobs and provide fast, cheap transportation for low-income neighborhoods.

Born in Barbados, Cummins immigrated to America in 1971 and found work as a skilled machinist, saving money so he could one day start his own business and put his two children through college. In 1990 he took a part-time job driving a commuter van, an experience that inspired him to eventually establish his own transportation service, Brooklyn Van Lines.

After his applications were twice rejected by the New York City Taxi and Limousine Commission—each time without any reason being given—a grimly determined Cummins finally received approval on his third try. The final hurdle was a vote by the council committee. Cummins arrived at the hearings in November 1996 armed with 938 statements of support from Brooklyn community groups, business associations, churches, and ordinary citizens all testifying that van services were a necessity in their neighborhoods because public busses were too expensive, rarely on time, unsafe, and traveled inconvenient routes.

City councilwoman Una Clarke, who represented the Brooklyn area in which Cummins would operate, testified before the committee that the regulatory system "has come up with new rules and new regulations to thwart Cummins . . . these vans represent economic development in my district." She pleaded, "They will help the poor women who otherwise would not have protection at night when they go to and from work."

The hearing room was packed with city bus drivers from the Transport Workers Union, which opposed lower-cost van services because they compete with the taxpayer-subsidized public transit monopoly. The union had made sizeable campaign donations to members of the committee, and their allegiance quickly became clear. "I plead guilty to protecting union jobs," declared councilman Archie Spigner, "The backbone of my community is made up of members of the Transport Workers Union who have good jobs with good wages and I don't want to see them competing with people who are much worse off." Moreover, Spigner charged, Cummins' van service would "provide the opportunities for desperate workers to be exploited and to exploit themselves."

By an 8-0 vote the committee rejected Cummins' license application. The hearing room erupted in cheers and applause as the transport union members celebrated another victory at thwarting competition.

We need look no further than this incident for an illustration of why the bottom rungs of America's economic ladder have become too slippery for many low-income entrepreneurs. An array of confusing regulations restricting economic activity have been put in place by city and state governments, usually on the pretext of protecting public health and safety, though the real motive is usually to protect special interests from the effects of honest competition.

"These sorts of regulations are widespread, and even the most modest occupations are very heavily regulated," observed Howard Husock, director of case studies at Harvard's John F. Kennedy School of Government, "There are economic advantages for certain entrenched groups to have many of these regulations which act to criminalize the work of low-income entrepreneurs. That is an invitation to corruption."

Government-sanctioned monopolies in mass transit date back to the early part of the twentieth century when "jitney" services first emerged as a low-cost competitor to electric street railways. Jitneys began operating in Los Angeles in 1914 with Model T autos picking up passengers for a nickel, or a "jitney," as the coin was known at the time. Within a year, an estimated 60,000 jitneys served 175 American cities, gaining popularity largely because they were faster and more efficient than streetcars. Alarmed by the competition, streetcar companies used their political influence to convince city governments to impose restrictions, even outright prohibitions, on jitney services. According to economists Ross Eckert and George Hilton, who have extensively studied the phenomenon, by the mid-1920s these regulations had eliminated nearly all jitneys nationwide.

Most streetcar companies evolved into private bus companies, and most of these in turn were taken over by local governments in the 1950s and 1960s. The public bus agencies and their unionized employees have helped maintain the restraints on jitneys in most major U.S. cities right into the twenty-first century. A Federal Trade Commission study in 1984 concluded that the effect of these regulations, for which "there was no economic justification," has been to "impose a disproportionate impact on low-income people."

Transit regulations are usually complex and compliance is expensive. Consider the process that frustrated Vincent Cummins in New York City. Three separate types of licenses are required for van owners to provide even limited services. In addition, the city prohibits vans from operating on any public bus routes, a devastating blow to would-be competitors since most main thoroughfares double as bus routes. Van services providers must prove that "present or future public convenience and necessity" demands their presence, which means petitions must be gathered from potential service users. But if the municipal bus line objects, as it almost invariably does, then van operators must demonstrate that existing mass transit is inadequate. That means interviewing hundreds of residents, as Cummins did, to gauge and record their opinion of public transit services. Even after all of this, city regulators can still veto van service simply by failing to act for 180 days after the application is submitted. Moreover, the city council can vote to deny a license, and in 98 percent of the cases it did just that.

To meet public demand for their services, which charged two-thirds what city buses cost per ride, most van operators have had to work without a license. That subjects them to city and state transit inspectors who write up fines of $1,000 and more and can confiscate the vans if they pick up or discharge passengers along bus routes. A New York City police captain boasted to the city council that his department had seized 424 vans in one three-month period, and some vehicles were impounded and sold by the city.

Sacrificed in this regulatory squeeze are the lives of hard-working low-income persons struggling to stay off the welfare rolls. Stewart Sutherland was laid off from his department store job and as a last resort took a job driving an unlicensed van. Sutherland saw firsthand how important his service was to the public when blizzards shut down the New York City bus system in the winter of 1996. Illegal vans continued to operate and ferried thousands of stranded workers to and from their homes and jobs. On one trip Sutherland was amused to find he had picked up thirteen municipal bus drivers and mechanics trying to get home through the deep snow.

"We don't want handouts or welfare," insisted Sutherland, referring to himself and other van drivers. "We want to make an honest living. We offer a service the public system can't. The people in this community want us here. Why can't the regulators leave us alone?"

The Institute for Justice took up the van driver cause in state court by seeking legal protection for their right to economic liberty. In early 1999, the New York State Supreme Court responded with a ruling that the city council cannot veto specific van operator licenses approved by the New York City Taxi and Limousine Commission. Two other sections of the local law were also struck down by this decision: one that automatically denied van applications not acted upon within 180 days, and another that had allowed the regulators to deny licenses without any justification being cited.

Left intact by the courts, however, were numerous other arbitrary and unreasonable burdens on the ability of van operators to provide competitive services. Vans are still prohibited from picking up or discharging passengers on city streets where public buses operate, and van riders must continue phoning ahead for van service rather than hailing vans from curbside as they would taxi cabs. None of these regulatory impositions have any real connection to genuine public safety concerns. They are simply designed, now with the court's blessing, to give city transit workers a continuing competitive advantage.

The Denver Taxi Drivers

"One of the most popular and time-honored trades for people seeking unskilled entrepreneurial work is to drive a taxicab," Howard Husock, a professor at Harvard's JFK School of Government, has observed. Driving a taxi has been called the poor man's gateway to mainstream America, and that is just what Leroy Jones, an African-American, and three other men, all African immigrants, wanted to prove by becoming successful entrepreneurs, while in the process providing much needed service to their low-income community in Denver, Colorado.

Jones had driven a Yellow Cab for two years but left after a dispute with the company over its treatment of drivers. With his three partners, all experienced taxi drivers, Jones formed Quick Pick Cabs, Inc. But a huge impediment stood in the way of their entrepreneurship. The Colorado Public Utilities Commission had prohibited entry into the Denver taxicab market to every applicant since 1947, thus preserving a monopoly for three existing cab companies. None of these companies, Jones contended, ever provided consistent or quality service to Denver's minority and low-income neighborhoods.

To get permission to operate, they would have to prove not only that existing taxi services were inadequate, but that the three existing companies were incapable of providing such service, a finding that could only be made if Jones and his friends financed an expensive economic analysis and survey study of Denver's transportation industry. Even then, the three entrenched cab companies could still thwart the emergence of competition by claiming that a new company would duplicate current services, a claim the commission had always responded to by denying new applications.

Sure enough, when Quick Pick filed its application with the PUC, all three existing companies filed protests. They served Jones and his partners with a series of burdensome requests for information specially designed to raise the application costs, inquiring about everything from details about Quick Pick's five-year advertising plan, to requesting the names of 100 persons driving taxicabs for one of the three companies who had sought work with Quick Pick Cabs if it received approval to operate.

In November 1992, the PUC denied Quick Pick's application for a certificate of public convenience and necessity. Jones and his partners simply could not afford to play a game in which the rules were stacked against them, so they joined with the Institute for Justice in 1993 and filed a lawsuit against the PUC challenging the constitutionality of the monopoly. No one had ever brought such a high-profile lawsuit before. The Colorado legislature responded to the prospect of losing its control to the courts by taking the initiative to lift the regulatory restraints on taxi competition.

In January 1995, Jones and his partners were granted fifty new permits for their company, the appropriately named Freedom Cabs. Seventeen months later a journalist for the *Denver Post* was inspired by the outbreak of competition to write, "For the cab-riding public there is clearly more choice, more cabs, more cab companies, and new types of taxi services."

The Nevada Limousine Drivers

William Clutter hoped his ticket to financial self-sufficiency would be the limousine he used to provide a shuttle service for Las Vegas tourists, celebrities, and visitors in town to participate in local weddings. One night in December 1997, as the thirty-seven-year-old Clutter was leaving a restaurant, the valet informed him that a man and woman wanted to catch a ride with him back to their hotel. Clutter agreed to drive them for free, something he did periodically as a courtesy to the restaurant because it provided him with frequent business from their patrons.

Once at the couple's hotel, two agents of the Nevada Transportation Services Authority (TSA) confronted Clutter, issued him a criminal citation, and impounded his limousine. As it turned out, Clutter's two riders were undercover TSA investigators conducting a sting against him. He was charged with "operating a carrier in intrastate commerce without a certificate of public convenience and necessity."

Up until two months previous, independent "uncertified" limo drivers like Clutter were left alone to operate so long as they did not advertise for business. They relied upon restaurant, hotel, and word-of-mouth referrals. Then, under pressure from the local monopoly of several large limousine companies, TSA asked for and received additional powers from the Nevada legislature to crack down on entrepreneurial drivers like Clutter.

At an impoundment hearing four days after the seizure of his limo, the TSA assessed Clutter criminal and civil fines of $5,000, and ordered that his vehicle be held in an impoundment lot indefinitely, racking up "storage costs" of $15 a day. Without even the courtesy of notifying Clutter, the TSA sold his limousine at an auction on February 14, 1998. When Clutter's attorney challenged the legality of this sale, TSA repurchased the limo and returned it to the impoundment lot, where it eventually sustained both internal and external damage, along with the loss of its license plates and registration papers.

A year passed and Clutter's limo was still being held by TSA, held hostage by over $5,000 in accumulated impoundment fees. Clutter now faced personal bankruptcy because he had to continue making insurance and vehicle purchase payments on the limo.

Why didn't Clutter simply apply to TSA for certification? He tugged at his beard and managed a grim smile before answering my question. "The whole TSA regulatory system is designed to protect the large entrenched companies and to prevent small entrepreneurs like me from competing."

Consider what happened to a fellow driver, John West, who filed an application for certification with TSA on September 23, 1997. The twenty-five-year-old wanted to operate his limo within Las Vegas, having already secured federal approval to operate as an interstate service. Approval of his application by the Federal Highway

Administration had taken only ninety days. But under Nevada law, in order for West to receive approval to operate, he had to prove that "the granting of the certificate will not unreasonably and adversely affect other carriers operating in the territory for which the certificate is sought."

During the application process, previously certified limo companies are allowed to pose questions and raise objections that the applicant must answer, no matter how long this delays the process, and no matter how much it might cost the applicant. Over the next year West answered four detailed requests for information from TSA, and five more requests from two certified companies, totaling more than 1,000 pages of data. The requests ranged from business, driving, and limo maintenance records, to a list of clients and prospective clients.

"I was shocked and angry," West recounted, "TSA forced me to turn over my client list allowing my competitors to go after my business. In what other profession does someone have to sacrifice his business in order to go into business?"

With a wife and two young children to support, West struggled along doing other jobs to raise the $15,000 he had to spend on this application process that was clearly designed to frustrate the applicant. In the previous two decades, only three new applications to provide limo services were ever granted for the Las Vegas area. The two largest companies allowed to operate—Bell Trans and Presidential Limousine—both lodged objections to West's certification, though neither had any limitation on the number of limos they could keep on the streets. Together the two companies operated more than 400 vehicles. What conceivable economic threat could a single limo operated by West possibly pose to these large companies?

TSA officials put up a smokescreen about their regulatory intent, claiming their regulations were designed to protect the public interest and public safety. Yet, both Clutter and West passed personal background checks and their vehicles repeatedly passed safety inspections. Rich Lowre, president of the Independent Limousine Owner/Operator Association, a group of fifty limo drivers who simply wanted a chance to compete, pointed out in public forums how the regulatory deck was stacked, and has always been stacked, to stifle competition, thus making transportation the single business activity in this gambling mecca where public choice was limited. Lowre also spoke from personal experience. The regulations forced him out of the limo business and he had to take a job delivering newspapers to survive.

For more than two years, West tried to navigate the application process before finally being rejected by TSA in April 2000. The grounds on which the agency based its decision were laughable. West could not prove to TSA's satisfaction that "he had enough money to go into business." Disgusted with TSA and its stranglehold on the economic fortunes of people like himself, West and his family moved to New Mexico where he took a job as a car mechanic.

Bill Clutter continued to fight the issue on grounds of economic freedom. "We aren't against regulation which insures that operators have a valid driver's license, insurance, vehicle inspection, and a criminal background check. But the government should have no right to tell honest citizens what their economic choices are. They've made criminals out of hard working entrepreneurs."

In an attempt to crack open this market, the Institute for Justice filed suit on May 4, 1998, against TSA and the state of Nevada. The state court suit argued that independent limousine operators were being deprived of the right to earn a livelihood without due process of law. During their many months of work in the discovery process, Institute attorneys Deborah Simpson, Dana Berliner, and Clark Neily, took the depositions of eight TSA agents, and at the height of the winter, using a flashlight, sifted through boxes of forgotten state documents pertaining to TSA stored in a dark and unheated warehouse. Expert witnesses were hired to produce extensive reports on the limo business in Nevada. The labors of these Institute attorneys generated a veritable mountain of evidence demonstrating that TSA protected a monopoly on behalf of the major limo owners, a monopoly designed to keep their profits high by stifling even the threat of competition.

Three years after the filing of the lawsuit, a Nevada district court judge vindicated the limo operator's right to economic liberty by ruling that their due process rights to earn a living under both the Fourteenth Amendment and the Nevada Constitution had been violated. Judge Ron Parraguirre concluded on May 16, 2001 that the TSA's intervention process "amounted to an onerous and unduly burdensome process by which the applicants were forced to either withdraw their applications, agree to limit the scope of their proposed operations, or incur increasing litigation fees and costs, in order to comply with the numerous financial information and disclosure demands made by the TSA as well as the intervening carriers."

Within hours after the ruling, a last-minute bill was introduced in the Nevada legislature, backed by the major limo owners and casino interests, which sought to cap the number of limousines in Las Vegas and perpetuate the limo cartel. The bill passed the state senate but died in the assembly because it failed to reach a vote before the legislature adjourned for the year.

For many of the former independent limo drivers the judge's ruling came too late. John West, who moved out of state with his family, summed up their frustrations: "I gave up three years of my life and my whole savings to this process. It is great to know it wasn't for nothing. Even though it won't help me, at least no one else will have to go through this again."

CONCLUSION

A Legislative Formula for Fairness

REGULATORY MEDDLING HAD SO DISTORTED the transportation industry in Indianapolis, Indiana, that a local newspaper reported in 1994 how someone could rent a stretch limousine-complete with television, VCR, and wet bar-for the trip to and from the airport, and do so at half the cost of a taxicab ride on the same route. The taxis were also dirty and poorly maintained, with service so erratic that even Mayor Stephen Goldsmith once waited two hours for a cab.

After becoming mayor, Goldsmith discovered to his surprise and dismay the existence of thousands of city regulations that were either outdated or unreasonably burdensome. One impact had been that low-income persons suffered more harm than other economic groups. "Denying business opportunities is bad enough," Goldsmith declared, "but to do it to the very people who need entrepreneurial opportunity is downright shameful."

Taxis became Goldsmith's first target for deregulation because entry was tightly controlled, with a ceiling of 392 taxi permits, of which two-thirds were directly or indirectly owned by a single operator protected from competition by city regulations. By preventing low-income entrepreneurs from entering the transportation business, low-income neighborhoods received poor cab service or no service. A twelve-member regulatory study commission appointed by Goldsmith reviewed taxi and other city regulations to determine their economic necessity, and recommended elimination of the ceiling on taxi licenses, an end to price fixing and entry restrictions, and the legalization of jitneys. In May 1994 the city/county council approved these proposals.

Within five months of liberalizing taxi regulations, taxi fares had plunged as a result of the formation of twenty-nine new taxi companies and one jitney van service, most owned by minorities and women. "Nearly overnight the dress code for taxi drivers went from ripped t-shirts to collars and ties," Goldsmith later reported. "Cabs are noticeably cleaner, cabbies are friendlier, and their vehicles are more visible on our streets."

As a next step, the commission examined all city licensure regulations and found widespread burdens on ordinary citizens. Many of the required permits were frivolous or absurd. Bar and restaurant owners, for instance, were required to obtain a license to keep a shuffleboard game on their premises. In response to these commission findings, the city/county council abolished 10,182 of 13,482 annual licenses and permits, including those required for milk cows, group dancing, junk peddlers, and pet shops. The building code was reformed to eliminate all low-impact permits, such as the one that forced homeowners to obtain city approval just to replace a door or window.

Few cities have been blessed with elected officials able to summon the vision, much less the political will, to initiate the sort of widespread deregulation that occurred in Indianapolis. Yet, the seeds for change exist in every community in the form of persons with legitimate grievances against regulatory abuse. These victims of overregulation are a force waiting to be harnessed by property rights reformers seeking public office.

As evidenced by progress made by the Institute for Justice and other legal groups dedicated to the defense of entrepreneurs and property rights, the nation's court system can be an effective and powerful forum for initiating and shaping reform. We are beginning to witness changes in the realm of property rights law approaching the historic level of Civil Rights and Free Speech decisions during the second half of the twentieth century.

Federal regulatory experts like former congressman David McIntosh of Indiana have seen misguided rules repeatedly trip up innocent homeowners, farmers, and small-business owners. To counteract this trend and add flexibility and common sense to the regulatory system, McIntosh proposed a reasonable three-step reform process. First, incentives need to be created for employees of regulatory agencies to work with citizens, without resort to threats or sanctions, to help them comply with the law. Second, those regulations found to be unnecessary, too costly, or duplicative should be abolished. Third, citizens need more procedural protections, especially the right to be presumed innocent until proven guilty. These steps should be implemented by all levels of government.

Here are other reforms for consideration.

- **Relieving The Private Burden Of Social Costs.** The legislated shifting of social costs onto property owners—especially for wetlands preservation, species protection, and the pursuit of affordable housing using rent control and other mandates—needs to be the target of aggressive legislative action to enshrine specific legal protections and levels of monetary compensation for affected property owners. "If society as a whole must start paying for the social purposes advanced by regulation, instead of foisting the cost onto people unlucky enough to own property," argues Harold Johnson, an attorney with the Pacific Legal Foundation, "a more balanced approach to government action will surely result."

- **Asset Seizures.** The presumption of guilty until proven innocent inherent in asset forfeiture laws needs to be overturned. It is a perversion of this nation's fundamental principles of justice for property owners to be in a position of being forced to prove their innocence of drug crimes to reclaim property local governments have seized based on mere suspicion. It is equally perverse and unfair for those very same local agencies of government to benefit from the sales of seized properties, an arrangement that gives agency employees every incentive to trump up charges, make false arrests, and otherwise corrupt our system of justice.

- **Eminent Domain.** So far, only a few state court systems have been applying the brakes on this expansive and coercive power of local government to enrich one private party at the expense of another. Legislative changes could help prevent future abuses. State and local governments should vote specific property owner protections into law, clearly defining "public use" to exclude any and all takings of private property that would benefit other private parties.

- **Regulatory Ombudsmen.** Every regulatory agency of government, be it federal, state, or municipal, needs an independent advocate for those under agency jurisdiction, much like the ombudsmen (taxpayer advocate) positions the U.S. Congress legislated for creation within the Internal Revenue Service. Such "advocates for the regulated" within regulatory agencies should be empowered with sufficient authority and legislative protections to intervene in agency decision-making to insure that fair applications of the law, and not bureaucratic egos, enforcement quotas, and legal precedent-setting, motivates those decisions that wield the coercive powers of government.

Ultimately it will be up to elected governments at the federal, state, and local levels, under pressure from concerned readers like you, to restore our collective faith in a regulatory system that has eroded its own trustworthiness. We are a nation of laws, yet the foundation of respect for them must always depend on fairness, not fear.

APPENDIX
Resources for Fighting Back

AMERICA IS BLESSED WITH A WIDE RANGE of aggressive public interest legal foundations dedicated to economic liberty and the protection of private property rights. Seven of these organizations are featured here as resources to draw upon in case you or someone you know becomes ensnared in the regulatory quagmires of federal, state, or local government.

INSTITUTE FOR JUSTICE
Mission Statement

Founded in 1991 by attorneys William "Chip" Mellor and Clint Bolick, the Institute describes itself as "our nation's only libertarian public interest law firm," pursuing "cutting-edge litigation in the courts of law and in the court of public opinion on behalf of individuals whose most basic rights are denied by the state—rights like economic liberty, private property rights, and the right to free speech. Simply put, we sue the government when it stands in the way of people trying to earn an honest living, when it takes away individuals' property, when bureaucrats instead of parents dictate the education of children, and when government stifles speech. We seek a rule of law under which individuals can control their destinies as free and responsible members of society."

Representative Cases

- Transportation Cartels: a successful state court lawsuit forced the Nevada Transportation Services Authority to break the monopoly stranglehold it had preserved for three limousine companies in order to prevent competition by independent limousine drivers. (see page 122)
- Occupational Licensing: a successful lawsuit in California forced the state to loosen occupational licensing restrictions on African hair braiders. (see page 110)
- Eminent Domain: a successful lawsuit in New Jersey saved an elderly widow's home from confiscation by a state agency acting on behalf of a hotel casino. (see page 27)

Contact

Case Investigations at Institute for Justice
1717 Pennsylvania Avenue, N.W.
Suite 200
Washington, D.C. 20006
202-955-1300
www.ij.org

CASTLE COALITION

Mission Statement

This nationwide coalition of activists opposed to eminent domain abuses was organized by the Institute for Justice in 2002. The organization provides ideas, advice, support, and networking contacts to persons threatened with the loss of their homes or businesses as a result of eminent domain projects initiated by state and local governments.

Contact

Institute for Justice (see prior listing)
www.castlecoalition.org

PACIFIC LEGAL FOUNDATION

Mission Statement

Founded in 1973, Pacific Legal Foundation calls itself "the first public interest nonprofit legal foundation to devote its mission to protecting the individual and economic freedoms of Americans. PLF represents the economic, social, and environmental interests of the public in court while emphasizing private property rights, freedom from excessive government regulation, a free economy, balanced environmental policy, and nonwasteful, productive, and fiscally sound government. PLF selects its cases based on their public policy implications and their ability to set legal precedent that will benefit a large number of people."

Representative Cases

- Wetlands Takings: the U.S. Supreme Court ruled that a Rhode Island property owner, who was prevented from developing his eighteen acres of marshland, was entitled to challenge land-use regulations even if they were on the books when the property was purchased.
- Rent Control Takings: a U.S. district court ruled favorably that the city of Cotati, California, had placed an onerous financial burden

on the city's mobile home park owners by imposing rent controls on mobile homes.

- Building Permit Takings: a federal trial court awarded damages to two brothers whose building permit for a hotel in Pompano Beach, Florida was obstructed by the city for over a decade, in effect a taking of their property under the Fifth and Fourteenth Amendments to the U.S. Constitution.

Contact

Pacific Legal Foundation
10360 Old Placerville Road #100
Sacramento, California 95827
916-362-2833
www.pacificlegal.org

MOUNTAIN STATES LEGAL FOUNDATION

Mission Statement

Seeks to provide "a strong and effective voice for freedom of enterprise, the rights of private property ownership, and the multiple use of federal and state resources; champions the rights and liberties guaranteed by the Constitution in support of individual and business enterprises and against unwarranted government intrusion. Mountain State Legal Foundation undertakes nationally significant public interest litigation, throughout the country, on behalf of deserving clients who cannot afford to hire private counsel."

Representative Cases

- Clean Water Act Takings: a lawsuit before the United States Court of Federal Claims on behalf of a family-owned New Mexico corporation that was forced to cease operations of oil and gas well water disposal because migratory birds might have been using the area for nesting.

■ Private Property Access: case before the U.S. Court of Appeals for the Ninth Circuit on behalf of Montana landowners who have been forced by the state to open their lands along non-navigable rivers and streams to public recreational use.

■ Property Zoning Takings: before the Arapahoe County District Court, a claim by two property owners in Littleton, Colorado, that the city's refusal to zone their property amounts to a taking that requires just compensation.

Contact

Mountain States Legal Foundation
2596 South Lewis Way
Lakewood, Colorado 80227
303-292-2021
www.mountainstateslegal.org

DEFENDERS OF PROPERTY RIGHTS

Mission Statement

Established "to counterbalance the governmental threat to private property as a result of a broad range of regulations. We believe that society can achieve important social objectives—such as protection of our environment and preservation of our national heritage—without destroying property rights or undermining free market principles."

Representative Cases

■ Endangered Species Act Takings: the U.S. Court of Federal Claims rejected efforts by the Interior Department to throw out a compensation lawsuit by an elderly man who owns a lot near Mount Vernon, Virginia, located ninety feet from a bald eagle's nest. The U.S. Fish and Wildlife Service had prevented him from constructing a modular home on his land.

■ Land-Use Takings: the U.S. Supreme Court upheld a lower court ruling that a property owner in Monterey, California, who had been prevented from developing thirty-seven acres of land by the city based on a series of regulations, was entitled to compensation.

Contact

Defenders of Property Rights

1350 Connecticut Avenue N.W.

Suite 410

Washington, D.C. 20036

202-822-6770

www.defenderpropertyrights.org

SOUTHEASTERN LEGAL FOUNDATION

Mission Statement

A public interest law firm "which advocates limited government, individual economic freedom, and the free enterprise system. We look for cases in which our involvement can make a difference, not just to the parties involved, but also on the policies or issues that are in dispute. Southeastern Legal Foundation strives to protect the environment, but the environment can be protected without destroying the individual freedoms guaranteed by the Constitution. SLF strives to help individuals and businesses stymied by excessive government regulation. The Foundation will devote its resources to ordinary citizens in danger of losing jobs, property, or other rights because they lack the funds for protracted court battles."

Representative Cases

- Land Regulation Takings: won a landmark U.S. Supreme Court decision, Lucas v. South Carolina Coastal Council, declaring that a coastal property owner was entitled to just compensation when state regulation took away the value of his property.
- Public Use Takings: represented Cross Creek, Florida residents against state and local government attempts to create "public use" areas on their properties without compensation. In response to lengthy litigation, the state revised land-use regulations to assist property owners.
- Endangered Species Act: successfully argued in federal court for limitations on the Endangered Species Act when the Tellico Dam–TVA project was halted to protect the snail darter.

Contact

Southeastern Legal Foundation
3340 Peachtree Road NE, Suite 2515
Atlanta, Georgia 30326-1088
404-365-8500
www.southeasternlegal.org

WASHINGTON LEGAL FOUNDATION

Mission Statement

"By litigating precedent-setting issues in the courts and before government agencies, publishing and marketing timely and relevant legal studies, and ensuring maximum exposure for its free enterprise principles through its extensive communications outreach program, the Washington Legal Foundation shapes public policy and fights activist lawyers, regulators, and intrusive government agencies at the federal and state levels."

Representative Cases

- Land-Use Takings: represents Lake Tahoe property owners before the U.S. Supreme Court seeking compensation for the temporary taking of their land by the Tahoe Regional Planning Agency.
- Hotel Rate Takings: sought compensation before the U.S. Supreme Court in the case San Remo Hotel v. City and County of San Francisco, in which a hotel has been prohibited from renting all of its rooms to temporary guests because the city regulates room use in the name of affordable housing.

Contact

Washington Legal Foundation
2009 Massachusetts Avenue N.W.
Washington, D.C. 20036
202-588-0302
www.wlf.org

Acknowledgments

THIS BOOK OWES ITS EXISTENCE to a research grant from the Cato Institute in Washington, D.C., whose two guiding visionaries, Edward Crane and David Boaz, understood the importance of connecting libertarian principles and solutions to the real life stories of ordinary Americans who have been victimized by the excesses of government intervention.

Prior to Cato's participation, *Reader's Digest* financed most of my research documenting these horror stories. For this support I am grateful to Bill Schulz, the magazine's former executive editor and longtime Washington bureau chief, whose friendship, mentoring, and unwavering commitment proved invaluable. My thanks also goes to William "Chip" Mellor and John Kramer at the Institute for Justice, who brought many of the case studies chronicled in this book to my attention.

Most importantly, my appreciation extends to the several hundred people interviewed for this book, whose willingness to share details about their lives, their heartaches, their humiliations, and to do so publicly despite the prospect of ridicule or even retaliation, provide an inspiring series of profiles in courage.

A Note from the Author on Sourcing

BECAUSE MOST OF THE STORIES in this book were originally researched and written for *Reader's Digest*, which published them in condensed form, the factual details, quotes, court documents, and internal agency records that I gathered for each story underwent rigorous scrutiny by the magazine's fact checking department to insure accuracy and fairness.

Index